RESTORING ANTIQUE TOOLS

HERBERT P. KEAN

The mythical Phoenix bird that rose
up out of its own ashes to live again

Astragal Press   *Mendham, New Jersey*

MW01285749

Published by

The Astragal Press
P.O. Box 239
Mendham, NJ 07945-0239

Copyright: Herbert P. Kean, 1998

Cover Photo by: Robert Garay
Cover design by: Donald Kahn
Sketches by: Herbert P. Kean

Library of Congress Catalog Card Number 00-112131
ISBN 1-879335-98-0

Printed in the United States of America

TABLE OF CONTENTS

OTHER TOOLS

CLEANING AND REFINISHING

ACKNOWLEDGMENTS

It's very rare that a technical book can be written without the author receiving some help from other specialists. This book is no exception. The men that edited this book are among the best in their individual fields. They kept the author's errors to a minimum, in addition to contributing helpful additions to the original manuscript.

My sincerest thanks go to:

HANK ALLEN

CHUCK GRANICK

JACK WHELAN

INTRODUCTION

WHEN TO RESTORE

The term **restoration** invokes some thoughtful arguments concerning antiques, or in our case — tools. There are some who believe that a tool should *never* be changed in any way, as that will destroy its integrity. There are others who feel that any change is OK as long as it makes the tool usable. I like to think that somewhere in the middle, where all the variables are taken into account, is the best place to be. What are these variables? Not more than what common sense would dictate:

1) If the tool is rare and there are only a few examples available for review and documentation, then changing something might forever lose the original size, shape, color etc. However, if a part of that tool is missing, and a properly documented description or picture of the part is available, then it becomes a matter of personal preference whether to have the part correctly reproduced or not.

It is my feeling that under these circumstances the part *should be* reproduced, particularly if its absence creates any confusion as to its function. It can be marked in a non-prominent place, with the date that it was replaced. Then, if it was not properly reproduced, future scholars will be able to reject it.

An example of this would be a missing wedge from a valuable molding plane. Even if the wedge is copied exactly, it may have been copied from a different period of the maker, and could cause future confusion. If it is not copied exactly, because of abuse to the original wedge or lack of skill of the restorer, it might very easily cause confusion. Marking the repro will certainly eliminate this problem.

Most collectors hesitate having this done as they fear it will reduce the value of the tool for a later sale. Tool collecting is getting to the point where the *serious* collectors are knowl-

1

edgeable enough to spot the repros anyway. And, the dollar difference between the real part and the repro, in the *non-serious* pieces, is not that significant.

2) Common or low value tools with missing or damaged parts can very easily be made usable with replaced or reproduced parts. By so doing, the tool is put back into the hands of a craftsman and given further life. An example would be a fine chisel with a handle replaced from a lesser valued chisel. Cannibalizing (replacing with a like part from a similar tool), is a very common practice for "working" tools. However, in more valuable tools, this can create problems for the researcher if the part is not of the same vintage as the rest of the tool. This occurs mostly in iron planes where different variations of the same model are available, as with Stanley, Sargent etc.

Therefore, cannibalizing valuable tools should be done only by those who understand the subtle differences between the various types within any model. There are some who believe it should *never* be done, regardless of the tool's value. They are concerned that it will confuse future typing of the many various models. To me it's a trade off: I would prefer to see a working tool working, even if it has a part that belongs on a different type.

Today's researchers are talented enough to tell the difference between parts from dissimilar types, and they are providing literature that clearly defines these differences.

3) Tools that are neither common nor rare are our main concern, i.e. midrange. This is where most restorations occur. Many of them are done according to the concepts and feelings of the owner. Where these feelings are strong, they usually negate out any "right or wrong" way to restore, as the right of ownership becomes the important point. As the collector becomes more serious, he gives more thought to the *right* way.

4) Where a piece is non-functional, because of years of abuse, some maintenance should be tried to get the piece back into use. Sometimes the damage has gone beyond the point of economic repair. At this point, the piece is disassembled for parts or sold cheaply "as-is". Only if it is very rare, would it

warrant being kept in FAIR or POOR condition in a fine collection.

RESTORED CONDITION

I have been giving restoring demonstrations for years. I have always started off by stating the condition that I would like to see antique tools in, whether they are to be actually used or just displayed:

Antique tools should be in the same condition today as they were a hundred or more years ago in the hands of a prideful worker.

This doesn't mean they should look brand new. The slight nicks and dents and oxidations that occur with every day usage give the piece more "character". Many collectors deplore an overshined brass part, because it never really looked like that. Steel that appears as if it is chrome plated is also not in keeping with the criterion above. But it should be noted that antique tools that are in a *truly* NEW condition are eagerly sought after, due to their rarity.

Throughout the book, the restored condition of the piece will be that condition most accepted by collectors. In an effort to reflect all tastes, I will also describe other conditions, even though they are not necessarily the popular choice.

RESTORATION TECHNIQUES

The extent of the restoration depends upon the skill of the restorer and the equipment that he has available. It goes without saying that almost any tool can be restored if enough time and money are thrown into it. However, unless there is some sentimental or self-satisfaction reason to restore a tool, it probably won't get done if it isn't worth the expense to do it.

I will try to keep the restoration tips at a level that most collectors can accomplish. I don't expect everyone to have a wood lathe in his basement, or even a small power jointer. But if you are going to undertake the repair portion involved in restoring, it is best to have some simple power equipment. It is possible to start with just hand-held electric drills, and belt sanders, rather than the stationary bench types. (To get reasonable flatness with a hand-held sander, you should mount it upside down in a vise.)

There are many apartment dwellers who use only hand tools and still do nice work; but it obviously takes much longer. If time is a meaningful factor, I deem the motorized bench grinder or wire wheel a necessity. I find it inconvenient to work without a bandsaw, and suggest a small bench model to start.

Before you recoil in shock at the words, "belt sander" and "wire wheel", let me quiet your fear by explaining that these tools can be used without the damage that they have been accused of doing. Any tool in the wrong hands can destroy most anything. Unknowledgeable restorers have ruined good pieces with naval jelly, wire wheels, belt sanders, and polyurethane. This doesn't mean that belt sanders and wire wheels, when used with the proper grit or grade, can't produce excellent work. You can certainly forget about polyurethane or naval jelly! Where it's applicable I will explain the moderation needed for the various restoration techniques, and in many cases — the patience.

I won't be getting deeply into the details of wood or metal working skills. I must assume that the reader has basic skills in these areas. As such, the repairs should only be tried if the reader feels that he has the necessary knowledge and ability. In each case, I will simplify the effort as much as possible, but some repairs will still be considered risky.

Risk is an inherent factor in restorations. Any procedure that is not reversible is risky. That is: if you break something and cannot get it back the way it was, you have obviously detracted from its value. There will be times when things don't go the way you would like them to. The key here is your ability to recover. When working with old and corroded parts, you will find problems everywhere. When applicable, I will give "recovery techniques" which will help you fix your mistakes. No matter how good a restorer you are, don't expect to go mistake-free all the time.

SUMMARY

There are two great rewards that come from restoring:

1) You will have the satisfaction of taking an ill-treated piece, and like the mythical Phoenix bird, have it rise up out of its own ashes to live again, and

2) you will be increasing the value of your collection, both aesthetically and monetarily.

I hope that this book will help you achieve these rewards, at least to some degree.

Note: The sequence of tools will follow the same order that is in *Collecting Antique Tools*, (Astragal Press).

BORING TOOLS

DRILLS

BOW DRILL:

The main problem with most bow drills is that there is only the drill; the bow is not there. The restoration is obvious: make a bow.

The easiest way is to cut the shaft of the bow from a thin piece of hardwood, $\frac{1}{8}$" to $\frac{3}{16}$" thick by $\frac{3}{4}$" wide by 29" long. Here is where a band saw or a jointer comes in handy. Of course you can always hand plane it to size. It should be cut from maple, hickory or ash if you want a strong springy bow. Taper it toward the tip if you are not getting the spring you need.

Cut two other pieces $\frac{1}{4}$" by $\frac{3}{4}$" by 5", and glue them to the end of the 29" shaft. You can cut the bow completely out of one piece if you prefer. File and sand the handle, rounding the corners as much as you like.

All that is left to do is to fit a string or thong from the handle to the tip of the bow. The easy way is to just drill a hole in the tip of the bow shaft, and another one in the handle, a half-inch back from the junction of the shaft. Insert the string or thong (with the knots on one side of each hole), leaving enough slack to get one wrap around the spindle of the drill, see Fig.1. Finish off with stain and wax if you like, see page 104. Stain any new string with walnut stain to take away the raw look.

Another way is to use an old chisel handle instead of the primitive one described above. You will have to cut a slot into the handle to accept the bow. Should the handle have a ferrule you will have to remove it. Glue the two pieces together and finish off with stain and wax as above. See Fig.2.

Even though wooden bows were used, and advertised by some of the more prestigious distribution houses, you may

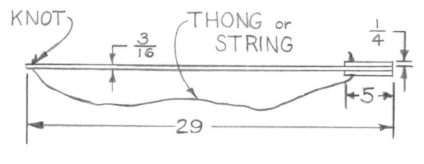

Fig. 1

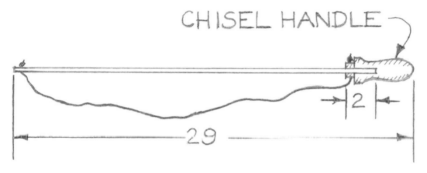

Fig. 2

wish to make a steel bow with a better matching handle. You will need a wood lathe for the handle. The bow can be made from a fencing foil that you can purchase quite reasonably at a flea market, particularly if there is only a single foil and it is of the common variety.

Disassemble the shield and grip from the foil, and cut the tang down to the size needed for your handle. Turn the handle on your lathe to match the bow drill handle. You can go back to using a chisel handle if you choose. Drill a hole 2½" - 3" deep in the handle to fit the tang, and epoxy it in. Use two-part epoxy from the hardware store.

Cut the foil back to around 26" out from the handle. With a small propane torch (available from the hardware store or factory supply house) heat the new tip until it is cherry red. Then bend it into an "S" as shown in Fig.3. Make a hook from the piece that was cut off. Drill a hole into the handle to fit this

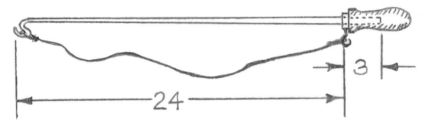

Fig. 3

hook about ⅜" back from the intersection of the shaft. Glue or epoxy it in. Cut the string or thong to take one wrap around the drill after it is affixed to the tip of the bow and the hook in the handle. Finishing can be done as in the previous example.

Although a missing bow is usually the main problem of the bow drill, the drill itself may have a few troubles of its own. The most common one is that the drill does not turn freely. If the spindle on the drill is a simple one, all that is generally needed is a little penetrating oil (*Liquid Wrench* or *WD-40* or the like) and some gentle turning back and forth. However, if the spindle is more complicated, similar to the grooved ones made in Sheffield, England and New York City, then disassembly is in order, though difficult in some cases.

Once apart, the shaft that seats in the handle of the drill can be cleaned and oiled, and all the threads likewise. By adjusting the locking nuts, the right amount of axial play (vertical clearance between the handle and the spindle) can be achieved. This clearance should be equal to the thickness of a business card, or at the most a credit card.

The bow and drill can be cleaned per pages 100 through 109.

The more sophisticated drills take tapered pads of brass that lock the bit in with a screw. These pads can be turned on a machinist lathe, or on a wood lathe that has a compound saddle with in-and-out and left-and-right micrometer feeds. These compounds can be adapted to most lathes but are not easy to find. If the supply houses don't have them, try the used machinery shops.

The simpler drills hold the bit directly in the chuck or the spindle shaft itself, but many times are missing the wing screw that does the holding. Sometimes this wing screw is not just missing but broken off, with the remaining part "frozen" to the spindle shaft. What was done by the old craftsmen was to merely drill and tap a new hole on the opposite side of the chuck and put in a new screw. You can do that, or drill out the old broken part and retap the hole (with a larger tap if necessary).

PUMP DRILL:

Aside from cleaning, the other thing most needed is replacement of the missing or broken string or thong. It's fairly straightforward. Thread the string up through the bottom of one side of the crossbar, through the eye at the top of the spindle shaft, and then through the other side of the crossbar. Make sure that when the arm is at the bottom of its stroke it doesn't touch the flywheel. The string only needs to be knotted at the bottom ends of the crossbar.

The earlier pump drills usually have their bits inserted directly into the spindle shaft. There is generally a knockout slot in the shaft that enables the bit to be driven out with a drift (a thin tapered piece of flat steel that fits between the end of the bit and the top of the slot). The later pump drills have three jaw chucks or chucks with tiny wingscrews. Broken wingscrews can be handled as described for the bow drill above.

ARCHIMEDEAN DRILL:

The most common restoration needed for this type of spiral drill is to get a smooth reciprocating action of the spiral stem. First cleaning off the crud in the grooves, and then using a fine wire wheel, will do the job.

For those "Yankee"-type drills that have nickel plate over brass, and most of the nickel is worn off, you may want to give it a homogeneous look by abrading off what's left of the nickel with some fine emery paper. You can then polish the brass on a rag wheel with tripoli or red rouge, depending on the level of the luster desired. However, if there is enough nickel to start with, it can be polished with a rag wheel with little or no rouge.

Drills that do not have their "rotation switch" working (which determines whether the drill will turn clockwise, counterclockwise, or not at all) are rarely worth the trouble to restore. The disassembly and reassembly is fairly tricky and time consuming. Besides that, the internal parts are not easily repairable.

BEVEL-GEARED DRILL:

These drills can easily be taken apart and cleaned to make them run smoothly. Some paint touch-up will also help. I find the acrylics easy to use.

The wood, brass or steel can be cleaned as described on pages 100 through 110.

AUGER AND REAMER:

The wood is cleaned in the standard way (page 100) but the metal requires some patience on the wire wheel. It is not a good practice to try to get the metal shiny, as it will just end up blotchy with broken patina here and there. It is best to just get rid of the surface rust with some #3 coarse steelwool and burnish what is left with a fine wire wheel. Heavily rusted and pitted pieces should just be wiped with machine oil and sold as "wall hangers".

Barn beam borers take some work to get into shape as they are usually rusted and in some cases rotted. When the material is sound, they can be disassembled and cleaned. The wood will probably be best cleaned with a stripping gel as discussed on page 101. If the iron has lost all of its paint finish, it can be painted per page 111. If the lock that holds up the drive gear is missing (which is not unusual), a new one can be made from a piece of sheet metal, with a pair of tin snips and files.

BRACES

PRIMITIVE BRACE:

Most of these braces are quite old (18th and 19th century). It is not a good idea to make them look too new. If the brace has a gray weather-beaten look, light stain with some tung oil or wax is best. If it already has a nice looking patina, a little tung oil is probably all that is necessary.

The biggest problem with primitive braces is that many of them are missing a pad and bit. Individual old pads are available occasionally, but not often enough to depend upon purchasing them for replacements. Even if one of these old pads were available, it probably wouldn't fit the brace or match its form and patina. What then? Make one.

Try to pick the wood to match the body of the brace. Normally they are of beech or birch, and sometimes ash, apple or maple. If you don't know your woods well enough to select the proper species, get someone from one of the clubs or a local cabinetmaker to help you. There is a section on identifying tool woods in *A Price Guide to Antique Tools* from Astragal Press.

Match the form of the pad to the forward end of the brace. If it is round then the pad should be round; if it's octagonal then the pad should be octagonal; if the body has very heavy chamfers, then the pad should also, etc. The length and shape of the tang is dictated by the hole in the forward end of the brace. But, the front part of the pad that holds the bit is up to you for length. Make it whatever looks right.

The end of the pad that fits against the brace is generally either the same size cross section or slightly smaller. Again this is up to you as to what looks right. A small crosspin can be inserted in the end of the tang that sticks out slightly beyond the web of the brace. This is to prevent the pad from slipping out of the brace when it is removed from the drill hole. See Fig.4.

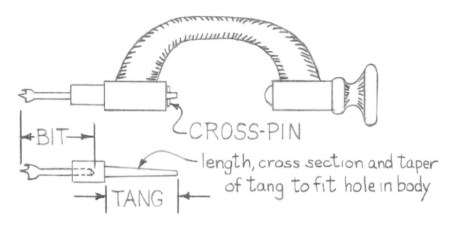

BIT
CROSS-PIN
length, cross section and taper
TANG
of tang to fit hole in body

Fig. 4

Finish off by drilling a hole into the pad for a bit, and forcing the bit into this hole. You could taper and square up the hole with a mortise chisel before inserting the bit. This will prevent the bit from spinning in the pad under heavy torque. If you choose not to be this correct, just fill the space between the round hole and the square bit with wood filler (after gluing or epoxying in the bit.) See page 104 for finishing.

SHEFFIELD BRACE:

These braces are of two distinct types, the unplated (usually earlier) and the plated ones. The plates are four pieces of thin brass, shaped to the web of the brace and screwed to each side of the front and rear webs.

Most of the time the screws are corroded to the wood, or the slots in the screws are "worn out" so as to make removal almost impossible without drilling out the screws. It is rarely worth it to do this. Unless a screw is missing, or the replacement is rather simple, I would suggest that the plates be polished only. The rag wheel is the best way to go. It should be done before the wood is cleaned so that run-over polishing marks can be removed when cleaning the wood. See page 100 for cleaning and polishing.

The most common problem that is found with these braces is a sloppiness between the head and the rear web. This comes from wear and a loosening of the internal nut that keeps the head on the spindle. It is a simple fix, but sometimes the disassembly is not so simple. In the center of the head is a threaded plug called a "trade disk". It has two small holes opposite each other through the centerline of the disk. These holes take the points of a spanner tool which screws the disk in or out.

Problems generally facing the restorer are:

1) not having the exact spanner tool to do the job, and

2) the disk being "frozen" tightly to the head, even with the right tool.

Here you'll face your first risky maneuver. Loosening a "frozen" threaded member is a real art form. You need to go step-by-step, starting with the least risky procedure and moving on to more risky ones (should the first ones fail). Many of these steps require "feel" to prevent broken parts. But even with all your skills available, there is still a chance for disaster. You must be prepared to accept this, OR DON'T START WITH THE PROCEDURE! In most cases, each of these chancy tricks has a recovery technique in the event they fail. But be ready for the worst.

The first thing *not* to do is flood the area with oil, even penetrating oil. Oil tends to swell wood and that is not what you want here. Penetrating oil is OK for a metal-to-metal problem, but not where wood is involved. If you do not have a spanner tool that fits, not to worry. Use a needle-nose pair of pliers. If by pressing downward (to keep the pliers from jumping out of the holes and scratching the disk) you are not able to turn the disk, then lock on to the pliers with a set of vise grips, see Fig.5.

Now with the added leverage, gently turn the wrong way, and then the right way, until it is broken loose. Short movements back and forth are best. Although this procedure is possible to accomplish without a vise, I don't recommend it. A woodworking vise and a metal working vise are really necessary items for a restorer.

13

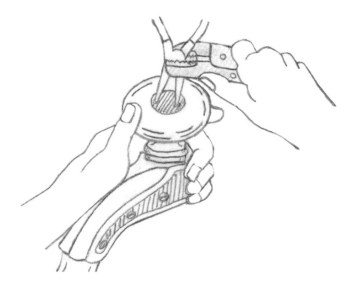

Figure 5

There have been very few times that this did not work. But there is one further technique to use even though it is somewhat drastic. With the head locked very firmly in the protected jaws of a vise, and with the grain running parallel to the jaws, insert a nail of the right size into one of the spanner holes. Tap the nail at the lowest point that you can in a counterclockwise direction. Patience — it may take more than just one tap, *and* it has to be a solid tap.

If even this fails, you can either give up, or tap the spanner hole directly with a nail punch. I have never failed to move a disk when using this last technique. Of course you will mar up the hole, and will have to drill *both* holes out larger to remove the mar (and make them equal). But these holes never were any particular size, so it will hardly matter. On with the repair.

After all that effort you would think that it would be a piece of cake from here on. NO — it could get worse. With the disk out, you will see a slotted nut, or two slotted nuts on top of each other, holding the head onto the spindle from the rear web. You will need another spanner tool to turn the slotted nut, and this time the needlenose pliers won't do.

14

If you don't have the tool you will have to make one from a piece of spring steel about .060 thick. A blade from an old rusty square or a metal rule might do. If the steel is too soft it will just twist up when heavy torque is applied. If it is too hard it will snap. The piece should be no more than ½" wide so that it will fit into the hole in the head, particularly when there is a deeper second nut. See Fig.6.

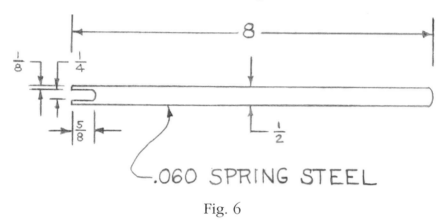

Fig. 6

Now, you can use penetrating oil, and also rap the top of the spindle to create some shock to the frozen part. If you need more leverage, lock vise grips to the spanner tool. Do not forget to press down and do the small back and forth movements described above. Many times, particularly in Ultimatums, the lower nut is left-handed and will require a *clockwise* motion to get it loose. That's why it's always good to go the wrong way a little when you are first starting out. It might tell you that the thread is left-handed. Whew! We finally have the thing apart.

Now, it *is* a piece of cake. Clean off the threads of the spindle with the wire wheel or a steel wire brush. Cut a leather thong just long enough to seat at the bottom of the counter-bore in the head, see Fig.7.

Put it all back together and check if the piece of leather is thick enough to take out the sloppiness between the head and the body. Crush the leather first and then relax it back. If it needs to be thicker, make a new piece. If it needs to be thin-

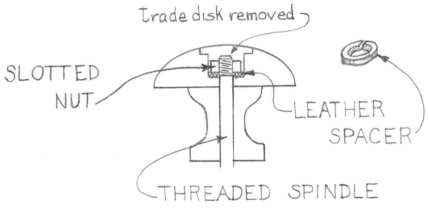

Fig. 7

ner, slice it back. Keep this up until the head turns smoothly with only a tiny bit of slop.

If there are two nuts, you can make sure that they stay locked at the position you want. With only one nut, it's a little harder to get it to lock. You may have to put a small spot of *Loctite* (a thread glue from Loctite Corporation, Cleveland, Ohio) on the nut.

The other major problem with a Sheffield brace is the chuck button. Sometimes it's stuck; sometimes it's missing. In both cases it's best to disassemble the chuck from the body. This is done by removing the chuck screw, which goes into one side of the chuck, through the body, and out the other side of chuck. Normally this isn't frozen, but when it is, it's not easy to remove. Penetrating oil, shocking blows, short back and forth strokes, etc. is what is needed.

Nine out of ten times this will loosen it. When the tenth time arrives, you will have to decide whether to give up, or drill it out. This will almost always require another screw. You can make a new screw if you have machine shop capabilities, or you can file and rethread one that is close. Feel good about the fact that it doesn't happen very often.

When you part the chuck from the body you can easily see why the button is stuck, and just as easily fix it. If the button is missing, you will have to make one. Hopefully, one of the standard brass rods will fit. If not you will have to find a friend with a lathe, or spend a lot of time filing and sanding it in the chuck of an electric drill. If you're lucky enough to have a standard rod fit, you can cut it to size with a hacksaw, then slit and pin it to the internal arm that holds the bit. To disassemble the arm from the chuck, remove the tiny square head screw. See Fig.8.

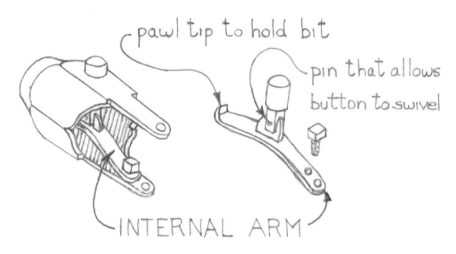

Fig. 8

BRASS-FRAMED OR "ULTIMATUM" BRACE:

The Ultimatum's head screws off from the neck. This gives you another place to get into the spindle if the disk is frozen. Most of the Ultimatums have ring chucks, which are very difficult to get into. To completely disassemble this style chuck, it is necessary to take the screws out of the frame and remove the infills. This also is what must be done if the wrist grip and the rest of the brace are loose from each other and "rocking around". The iron shaft that is through the wrist grip must be peened to the forward and rear frames. I don't recommend this unless you are fairly good with both metal and wood.

Sometimes the wrist grip doesn't spin very freely. You can work on this with a little oil and some back and forth movement. The sloppiness in the head can be fixed in the same manner as the Sheffield brace. The metal and brass can be cleaned in a similar manner also.

One thing that the ebony Ultimatums usually have is cracks. Here are a couple of ways to fill them: You can mix ebony sawdust and glue; you can mix ebony sawdust and epoxy; you can mix wood filler with ebony sawdust or lamp-black, or mix epoxy with lampblack. (I like the last one).

When the fill hardens and you have smoothed it off, you will most likely have to stain the finished surface to get it black enough. There will be times when the stain doesn't take, particularly when using epoxy. When this happens, use a *MARKO* pencil. You will have to practice "blending" the marko ink in with your finger. Let it dry at least a half hour before applying any surface finish.

Ultimatums almost always have an ivory ring in the head. Sometimes there are parts, or all, of this ring missing. The missing parts can be replaced with pieces of ivory flat-tened with sandpaper and cut to size with a jeweler's saw. The ends of these partial circles are cut square rather than on a diagonal to more closely portray the original piece that devel-oped cracks across it through the years.

Ivory can be stained with boiling tea or dye penetrants (see page 113) to match the aged pieces that are left. If there are not too many pieces left, you may find it easier to replace the entire ring. Of course this will depend upon whether you have the ivory to do it.

HANDFORGED BRACE:

These are the oldest of the iron braces and usually have a very dark patina. Do not scrub away at this surface to remove the oxidation. It is best to merely burnish it with steelwool and then apply machine oil.

The heads on these old braces are generally worn and loose. When the spindle is riveted to hold the head on, the repair is too invasive and time consuming to be worth it. If the head can be removed by unscrewing a locknut (counterbored into it), that might be worth it. Most of the time you will find these locknuts permanently frozen to the spindles. When that happens, give up and write it off to old age.

An easier problem to fix is a missing or broken-off wing screw that holds the bit in the chuck. This can be corrected similar to the way described for bow drills on page 9.

IRON PATENT BRACE:

These braces came into being in the middle of the 1800s. They all but replaced the hand- forged ones and the wooden ones by the end of the century. Many of them do not have a heavily oxidized patina and can be cleaned up to reflect a deep "pewter" look. A fine wire wheel will usually accomplish this. Be careful not to hit the wood of the wrist grip or the head with the wire wheel. If the head can be removed, that will make it much easier to clean. The wood can be cleaned as on page 100.

Some of the earlier patent braces have a wingscrew to tighten the bit in the chuck. Any repairs in this area should be done in the same way as those described on page 9. The later patented chucks are more complicated and usually need wire wheeling and oiling.

BIT:

The various bits that were used for the braces above can be cleaned on a wire wheel. They can be sharpened with a small carborundum stone. The tangs of these bits that are used in Sheffield and Ultimatum braces, and some early American patent braces, need to be notched to fit the pawl in the internal arm of the chuck. See Fig. 9. If you are not concerned with that degree of authenticity, you can merely pick a bit that has a good enough matching taper to friction fit to the chuck of the brace.

Many old bits have pieces of their tips broken away. It is rare that they can be properly restored. As these bits are easy enough to come by, find one that is correct. With a good sharp bit, and a functioning old brace, you'll surprise yourself with the degree of accuracy that you can achieve.

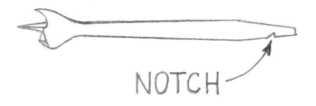

Figure 9

EDGE TOOLS

AXES

FELLING AXE:

Felling axes are generally of lesser value than other type axes, and as such are not always economically restorable. Let's assume you find a chipped edge, rusty head from a felling axe (no handle). It will take some time to grind out the chip, as you will have to proceed slowly so as not to lose the hardness of the edge. Then a good scrubbing with a course wire wheel to get rid of the rust. Then you have the cost of a handle, whether it is new or old, and the time necessary to fit the handle to the head, wedge it in, and blend it all together with stain and oil.

Unless the axe has quite a bit of historic value, or is collectible for some other reason, it won't come close to being worth the effort. Although many collectors do not place a value on their restoring time, some do. Those that do, get an added satisfaction when they upgrade the value of the piece proportionately more than the value of their time spent in doing it. However, if you are not efficient, counting your time might only result in discouragement. To each his own.

But let's consider a beautifully profiled Victorian fire axe, with embossing designating the maker or the fire company. NOW, we really have something. Assume the handle is broken off a few inches from the head. OK get to work.

Saw the handle off close to the head and drive it out. You'll need your vise for this. *Do not burn it out*, as a fire hot enough to destroy the handle will likely destroy the hardness of the blade (unless you go through the trouble of cooling the cutting edge while burning).

Hopefully, you have an old handle or two that you picked up in a flea market or garage sale. I buy them any chance I get, even if I have to take a miserable head along with a great handle and throw the head away. If you don't have an old handle that will fit, you will have to use a new one. Scrape the varnish off it and rough it up. You can go as far as distressing it with a hammer, screwdriver, chain, stones, you name it. Then stain it to give it some age. Tung oil or wax will help, unless we are dealing with a very old axe — then forget the wax.

Make sure the handle is "fat" enough where it will be fitted to the eye of the head. Either with a drawknife, spokeshave, or rasp, make the cross section of the handle match the eye. By driving the handle into the eye as you go along, you can see the scuff marks that denote where to take off more wood. When it is close to seating all the way, saw a slit in the handle for the wedge. The slit goes from front to back and is about three-quarters of the head depth. Now cut a wedge from hickory, ash, or maple. It should taper slowly and fill up the length of the slit. See Fig.10.

Figure 10

Before driving the wedge in permanently, make sure you are satisfied with the patina of the head, and the smoothness and color of the handle. You may want to burnish the handle with a hardened steel burnisher to get any open grain to close up. Tung oil won't hurt, particularly if it's an old handle.

When you feel right about the finish, drive the wedge in, saw it off, and distress the sawn off surface with a lot of hammer pounding. Then apply the same stain and oil that you used on the rest of the handle. Oil the head too.

Unless you've done this before, or are good at woodworking, there is a strong possibility that the handle won't fill up the eye in all the areas. Not to worry. Make some smaller

22

wedges to fit the "holes" and drive them in. Cut them off flush, stain them and you are done.

BROAD AXE:

Many broad axe handles are incorrect. In order for a broad axe that is "chisel-ground" (bevel-ground on one side only) to function properly it needs to have its handle swayed away from the head. This is to allow your knuckles to clear when squaring up timber. Some broad axes that are ground on both sides ("knife-ground") have straight handles, which are correct. But a straight handle in a one-side-beveled broad axe is incorrect. If this axe is one of the valuable broad axes, it would pay to replace the handle. If you can buy handles through catalogs (some are made in Appalachia) you should do so, as the time it takes to make one ends up more costly. Anyway here's how:

The proper way is to cut the handle from a bent piece or steam the bend in. Neither of these alternatives are very likely, so the next best way is to use an old pick axe handle. It will have a very large end that fits the eye of the pick axe. There is usually enough wood to cut the eye for the broad axe on a slant. See Fig.11. You won't get the full sway that is preferred, but it will do. As with all wood-fitting jobs, make the male part bigger than necessary, as you will need that extra wood to make up for any mistakes that you may make in your rough forming stage.

Almost all primitive broad axes were wedged between the eye and the handle, rather than down a slit in the handle as the more modern axes are wedged. Most likely you will have to fill some spaces between the head and the handle anyway, so plan on wedging the old-fashioned way.

Pick axe handles are quite long. But broad axe handles are not because the broad axe is not used with a full over-the-shoulder swing. Cut the handle off so there is about 16"-18" from the bottom of the head. Smooth and slightly round over the end that you cut off. Stain the handle walnut to give it an aged look.

23

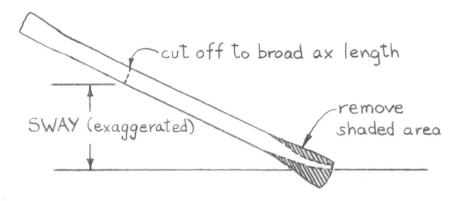

cut off to broad ax length

SWAY (exaggerated)

remove
shaded area

Figure 11

It is not advisable to try to remove all the rust. If you do, you might break through the patina and have a shiny spot. You can get off most of the rust with a medium grade steel-wool (No.1). If you're careful, you can work the blade over with a fine wire wheel instead of the steelwool. Don't hold it in the same spot too long or you will break through the patina. Use the side of the wheel for finer burnishing.

OK — you turn to answer your spouse who is advising you of a phone call, and uh-oh you have broken the patina. Well, at least you have someone to blame it on (if you think you can). What is needed now is a "recovery technique". And there is one. The spot needs to be chemically treated to quickly oxidize it back to where it was.

There are many chemicals that will do this, but the ones that are the safest and the easiest to buy are in a gun store. Gun blueing and gun browning will work fine. Some require the piece be heated first, most do not. You can get many shades of color by experimenting with additional applications, or mixing the blueing and browning solutions. Different man-ufacturers give varying results, so try more than one brand. See page 110. Wear a face shield, and gloves. You will be sur-prised how the miniscule vapors from these chemicals attack the sensitive skin areas.

GOOSEWING AXE:

Goosewings are the top-of-the-line axes. Even though the handles for goosewings are quite difficult to replace, the effort is worth it if the head is in reasonable condition. American axes, mostly from eastern Pennsylvania, usually have the eye canted (slanted away at an angle) from the head. This takes away a good part of your work. You don't have to worry about carving a bend in the handle as you did for the broad axe. With European axes, mostly from Germany and Austria, you don't get off so easily. These axes usually have their eyes in a direct line with the head with no cant. Now you have to carve the bend in the handle.

If you are really interested in doing the job right, particularly if you want to replace more than just one of these handles, you should practice with a nice soft piece of thick pine, simulated to look like the top end of a pick handle. The reason for this is that you will be working in all three dimensions at once, and there is not much room for error. If you take away wood to match one side, you might change the angle of insertion and foul up something else. It has to go slowly until you get the hang of it. Leave the rust in the eye, so it can act as an indicator as where wood needs to be taken away.

It would be nice if you could make a plaster of paris or clay cast of the eye so that you wouldn't be working in the blind, but your cast won't draw out cleanly because of the very rough surface of the internal eye. Pieces of wood or cardboard for each of the angles will help. But nothing is better than actually practicing with a dummy piece of soft wood.

Let's be realistic. Your first attempt is probably going to show some open spots at the tip of the eye, where it is the narrowest. Don't sweat it. Make some contoured wedges that fit the open spots and drive them in at the very end of the handle. They will almost always hide your apprentice error.

The finishing of the handle and the blade can be done similar to that described for the broad axe.

TRADE AXE:

These axes, as their name depicts, were used mostly for trade with the Indians. As such, they were not of the best quality. The heads were usually handforged completely from iron without the steel edges that most axes of the period possessed. Later, when iron was cast, the axes were even of a lesser quality.

Even though the Spanish and the French put decorations on some of these axes, they paid little attention to the handles. Mostly these handles were from branches, with no attempt to turn them round. So if you are to replace a handle on a trade axe, don't make it "too good".

Although the belt axes of Indians *in the movies* glint in the sun, and shine even in the shadows, the real ones were mostly of low grade iron and oxidized dark. Only the higher grade pieces (and some obvious repros) show any shine.

TURF OR BOG AXE:

The handles on these axes were very much like the ones on trade axes, usually primitive. The heads had no steel edge as steel was not needed for cutting turf. The more primitive the handle, the better suited it is for a turf ax. But it has to look old and used.

ADZES

CARPENTER'S AND SHIPWRIGHT'S ADZE:

These tools had their handles set through the eye from the top down. This was to make it easier to sharpen by removing the head with a simple downward blow of the handle. Handles for adzes are sold in flea markets and in hardware stores along with axe handles. You will have to pick one that has a full enough tip; that will not go through the eye when fully seated. If the head doesn't completely seat, you will have to take off some wood using a drawknife or rasp. When properly matched to the head, the handle should be finished similar to an axe handle.

HAND ADZE, BOWL ADZE AND COOPER'S ADZE:

There are a variety of ways of seating the head to the handle: with a wedge as in the stirrup style hand adze; in a socket as with the cooper's adze; and in an eye as with early bowl adzes. In each case, keep in mind that these handles are short, around 6" to 8" out from the bottom of the head (including the socket). The early handles were hand-carved to shape, but the later ones were factory turned.

Because these tools were sometimes used for digging, the edges can be pretty chewed up. When sharpening, always put the bevel on the lower side toward the handle.

Some of the later factory pieces were made from good iron and steel and can be refinished to a smooth "pewter-looking" surface. The handle is finished similar to all axe and adze handles.

CHISELS AND GOUGES

CHISEL AND GOUGE WITH TANG OR SOCKET:

Tang chisels and gouges are set into a hole in the handle and a metal ferrule is usually fitted over the junction to keep the handle from splitting. Chisel handles are plentiful, both old and new. If the ferrule is missing, it is easier to find a different handle than to make a ferrule.

Socket chisels and gouges do not require ferrules on the juncture end, but do need them on the pounding end. These are just pieces cut from an iron pipe or tube, and not that tough to make. You might have to file down the end of the handle to give a tight fit.

The tapered part of the handle that fits into the socket can be too big (as in the new handles) or too small (as in worn old handles). The tapered part can be filed to size if it is too big. If it is too small, a sawcut will first have to be made all around the handle a little way up from the end of the taper. File off the wood between the cut and the end of the taper, maintaining the same angle of taper. File until it *almost* seats and then pound it home, Fig.12.

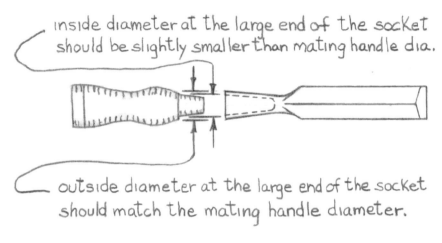

inside diameter at the large end of the socket should be slightly smaller than mating handle dia.

outside diameter at the large end of the socket should match the mating handle diameter.

Figure 12

If the steel at the end of the chisel is pitted, the edge is not usable. If the pitting can be ground away, do so. If the steel is in good shape, then a nice cleanup is in order. The newer chisels can be cleaned with emery paper and then a fine wire wheel. If there is no deep rust showing, the wire wheel will be all that's needed. What's left now is the sharpening.

There are as many ways to sharpen tools as there are woodworkers to sharpen them. The one classic way that has survived down through the years is below. I'm not saying it's the best, just the easiest:

1) If the edge is very dull or it's abused, clean it up on a grinder, either a wheel or a belt (a belt is easier). Cool the blade often by dipping it in water every few seconds. Don't allow any color to appear at the edge. If you do, you are ruining the temper. Don't stop the grinding until you can feel a slight burr all the way across the edge.

2) If the edge is not too abused, but just slightly dull, go over it with a rough India or Carborundum stone, rather than

the grinder. Once again, don't stop until you feel the burr.

3) Use a fine Arkansas or India stone to remove the burr. Go back and forth from the front side to the back until the burr is gone. *Be careful not to roll over the edge.* The stone and the surface that you are honing must be dead flat to each other.

4) If the burr is persistent, finish it off with a leather strop.

After a chisel is sharpened it can be toned up on a felt wheel to maintain its edge. This is something that you will need someone to show you how, as it is a finesse thing.

You will have to keep two things in mind when sharpening tools:

1) You can't make a "silk purse out of a sow's ear". If the steel is not very good to start with, you'll never really get a good edge. Ask an experienced woodworker to look at the steel if you're having trouble getting a decent edge. He may be able to tell its hardness from the ring it gives when passing over it with a file.

2) You cannot allow the stone to roll over the edge. The amount of roll that can dull all your fine efforts is almost infinitesimal. You will have to learn how to put the blade on the tip of your finger to prevent the stone from rolling. See Fig.13.

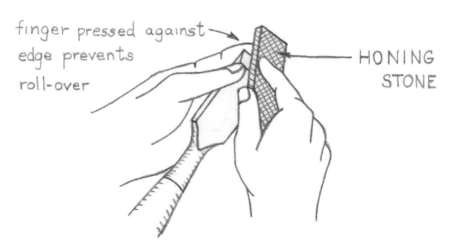

finger pressed against
edge prevents
roll-over

HONING
STONE

Figure 13

29

When you are using a stationary stone, the same pre-caution has to be taken to keep the *tool* from rolling. Get a magnifying glass to help you see the burr and the rolled edge.

You will need round tapered slip-stones for gouges. The same precautions apply. With a gouge you have the option of grinding the bevel on the outside of the blade (out-cannel ground) or on the inside (in-cannel ground). It's much easier to grind an out-cannel, but in-cannel is needed where a straight vertical cut is required, as in patternmaking or for a deep inlay.

KNIVES

DRAW KNIFE, SCORP, BLOCK KNIFE AND CHAMFER KNIFE:

There's not much difference in restoring any of these knives. They are probably all dull from abuse, and will need to be sharpened and honed as described above for chisels.

RIVING KNIFE (FROE) AND BARKING KNIFE (SPUD):

Although these are called knives they don't cut; they separate. A froe splits the wood along the grain and a spud separates the bark from the wood. In both cases, the blade should never be sharp. You do not want it to cut, or you will be defeating the purpose of the tool. So, if you see a froe or a spud with a sharp edge, dull it up, and dull it good.

CROOKED KNIFE:

These knives are for shaping handles and other similar uses. They were supposed to have been made *only* by Indians. I won't argue the point that *some* of these knives were made by Indians. But many were made by ship's carpenters, whit-tlers, and repro artists. They are always pulled toward the user, contrary to the good safe instructions of the Boy Scouts.

Aside from being dull, the other common malady of these knives is that the string or wire wrap that secures the blade to the handle is loose or unwinding. You can glue every-thing back (which is not the way it was originally done) or take off the old winding and rewind it, if the old stuff is good enough. If not, use new brass wire or string.

If the blade is worn loose, it can be epoxied back in place, although if you wind tightly enough, that should do it. To keep the ends from unraveling, "whip" them as shown in Fig. 14.

If for any reason the blade comes away from the handle, be careful when you put it back that the edge is on the proper side. Remember crooked knives are used pulling toward you, while your thumb rests in the shallow groove at the base of the handle (pointing away from the blade). I've restored a knife or two that had its blade in *backwards*, either from a prior improper repair or from a repro artist with no knowledge of how the knife was used.

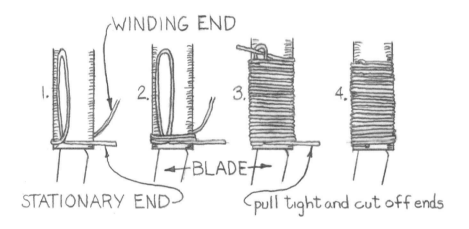

Figure 14

PLANES

Of all tools, planes are the ones that are most restored, probably because there are more of them than any other type of tool, but also because they are the tools that most collectors want. As the supply of fine tools dwindles, the desire to restore increases. If it is possible to take a piece that looks like the wrath of God and make it into a work of art, then why not do it?

The best restorers are smart enough to know how to do this without ruining the historic authenticity of the piece, and in many cases the restoration is so perfect that only "her hairdresser knows". Planes led the way in striving for correctness in restoring, and this concern has found its way into tools of all types. But, in the background lurks the lukewarm acceptance of replacement parts. In many cases, without them there is no restoration possible.

There are only two good options open today: restore as closely as skill will allow, or don't touch it. Even the serious "functionalists" will agree that there is no place for sloppy, careless restorations — at least not if the piece is to be considered a collectible.

WOODEN PLANES

Although there are many categories of wooden planes, it is best to break this section down by the major parts of the plane that are to be restored. Then they can apply to every group and subgroup in the same manner, and save a lot of space. These parts are: **body**, **wedge**, **fence and fence arms**, **thumbscrews**, **locking nuts**, **handle**, and **irons (blades)**. There are a few other parts such as skates, depth stops, etc. that will be taken up when needed, rather than handling them as a special group.

Throughout the book when replacement parts are to be made, try to use old wood from tools that are otherwise totally non-collectible and non-usable. Jointer planes are the best source for this. If you find a completely beat-up, un-signed yellow birch plane, grab it.

REMOVING THE WEDGE:

Before getting into the actual restoration, it might be wise to discuss the most frequently required disassembly: the removal of the wedge. Although the plane user of years ago was primarily interested in getting the wedge out of the plane to sharpen the blade, today's collectors have a different motive. They care about nicks or dents put into the wedge during its removal, because the collector's primary reason for disassembly is usually to improve the looks of the plane. Sharpening is only a secondary reason.

A common method to remove the wedge from a molding plane is to rap it on its finial while holding the body. You might argue that why else was the finial designed into the wedge. Well, I would agree that when the planes were used every day and the wedges were loosened once or twice a day, it was entirely possible to strike the finial with little damage to the wedge. But after a hundred years of laying in a barn and being almost permanently stuck to the body, striking the wedge as described above will usually cause some harm, and in some cases snap off the finial.

Better ways are:

1) With the plane upside down, hold the wedge in your hand and strike the rear of the plane with a mallet. See Fig.15.

2) If this fails, put the plane in a vise, holding it by the wedge and then strike the heel with a mallet. See Fig.16.

"Frozen" wedges are somewhat more difficult to remove from a bench plane. Usually they can be removed by striking the heel of the plane with a mallet while holding the plane on the bench, or striking the top of the plane about halfway between the nose and the throat. In some cases there is a strike button built into the plane at this point to provide a harder surface to hit. Without this button, many bench planes have torn-up tops from repeated pounding.

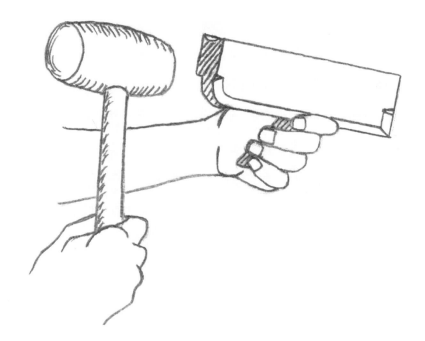

Figure 15

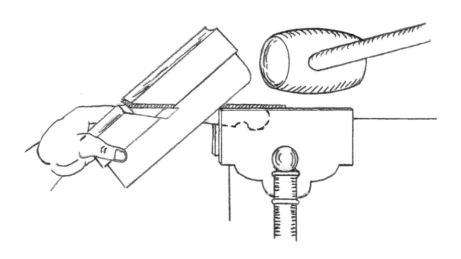

Figure 16

Badly-frozen bench plane wedges will not move even though struck over and over by the method above. You can try mounting the wedge in a vise as described for molding planes. If you get a good solid strike on the heel with this technique, the wedge will probably loosen. Many times that solid strike is elusive because of the length of the plane. There is another method that requires a little finesse and some patience but I have always gotten it to work:

Tap the sides of the wedge, (alternating sides) until a slight looseness is felt. Then wiggle the wedge back and forth and *upward* at the same time. Repeat tapping if needed. Give it a chance; it will work.

Where a tapered iron is present (either in bench or molding planes) tapping the iron deeper into the plane, to break any friction between the wedge and the iron, sometimes helps. If the wedge is badly swollen against the body, even this will not loosen it, and you will have to proceed with the methods above. If the iron is *not* tapered, you might make things worse by driving it deeper.

Remember, whichever method you choose to use, patience is the byword. Repeated shock and vibration will loosen almost anything. The trick is to apply them with care.

BODY:

WORM HOLES AND NAILHOLES:

These can be filled with some wood filler from the hardware store. I like *Plastic Wood* (which is the brand name) because it dries to the hardness that I prefer. It also comes in colors, and that helps a little. You may find other brands just as good. Always fill with more than it takes, so that you can smooth off when it dries. You will find that any of the stains that have volatiles mixed with them (such as alcohol) might eat some of the filler away. This might require you to go over it again with more filler. This time stain it with a Marko pencil.

CRACKS AND CHECKS:

These are usually handled in the same way as the holes above. Sometimes they can be closed up tightly with glue and clamps. The new glues today work wonders. I use "yellow" glue mostly (*Titebond* or others). Occasionally, more working time is desired before set-up. In this case use the "white" glue. Where a small chip breaks off while I'm working on something, I use "crazy" glue (cyanoacrylate- *Krazy Glue*). This glue will dry almost instantly. They now have some types that are used especially for wood.

Where tremendous pressure is needed to close up a crack, try the polyurethane glues,(*Gorilla Glue*). If the parts are clean and *wet*, these glues are terrific. You should always try to close up the cracks with glue first. If gluing doesn't work, then you can fill them.

CHUNKS MISSING:

When a large chunk is missing it is far more troublesome. Wood filler can be built up layer upon layer until the chunk is filled. Naturally each layer (appx. $\frac{1}{8}$" thick) should be thoroughly dry before the next layer is put on. It will be hard to mask the fact that the fill is synthetic. Even a good stain job won't completely hide it. The other alternative is to patch in a piece of similar wood with matching grain (called a "Dutchman"). Not easy, unless you are a good woodworker or carver. But it will look the part if you can do it.

RESURFACED SOLE:

A beat up sole, can be resurfaced. I do it on a power jointer, but if you don't own one you can use a stationary belt sander (or a portable hand-held one upside down in a vise). I hesitate to suggest trying a hand plane, unless you have some experience in that area. Finish it off with fine sandpaper, 0000 steelwool and then a burnishing rod. This tends to give a better base for the patina that you will be imitating later.

STAINS:

Stains are tough. If they are just surface stuff, the strippers discussed on page 101 will get rid of them. But if they go deep into the wood, you don't have too many choices. You can try to stain the rest of the body to match, or try to bleach it out. Oxalic acid in powder form is a mild bleach that works reasonably well for iron stains. There are more invasive bleaches in the hardware store. You will have to test these first, and above all follow directions.

BOXING:

Boxing, a narrow wear strip of boxwood (or rarely lignum vitae) is sometimes missing on molding planes, either partially or entirely. The original boxing was cut with the grain on a diagonal running from rear to front, Fig.17.

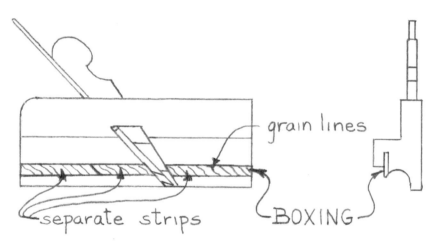

Figure 17

If you want to be completely authentic with the boxing, *and* you have boxwood that is wide enough to get diagonal grain, cut the strips as long as the width of the wood will allow. But, if the width is a problem, then cut the boxwood with longitudinal grain. Bring it to the thickness required for a nice snug fit in the groove in the sole of the plane. I always cut the diagonal ends to the boxing (where it crosses the mouth of the plane) before gluing.

Try them for correctness of the angle, and adjust the angle if slightly off. Do not cut the piece to the exact length before gluing in. Have the boxing strips stick out ½" or so beyond the toe and the heel of the sole. You can cut them to final size later. Meanwhile these stickouts provide a means of getting the strips in and out before gluing. They also give you a little grace for end-chipping as you shape the profile.

After gluing in, you can cut the profile of the boxing to match the pieces that are still in the plane. If *all* the boxing is missing, you will have to match the standard profile required by the plane. You can do it with planes, chisels and gouges, provided that you are a reasonably good woodworker. If not, hack away at it with rat-tail and flat files until you can smooth it up with sandpaper. See Fig.18.

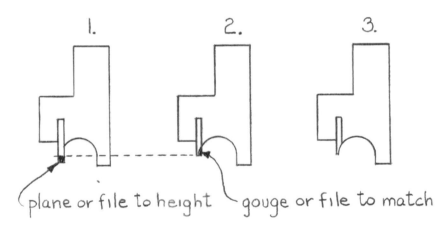

Figure 18

The boxing can be finished in the standard way for all wood, described on page 105. You may have to deepen the color of the replaced section with a marking pencil if the original boxing is very dark.

PLUGGING:

If a plane body was severely cracked, to the point where the user felt that it might not hold together, he would put a screw into the piece as a repair. It was ugly, but it did the job. If you wish to "repair the repair" you can try to get the screw out. More than likely it is corroded to the wood and will take quite a bit of effort to move it. If it hangs in there and you are insistent upon getting it out, turn to page 48 for more drastic methods of removing screws. After getting the screw out, glue the crack, and plug the hole that's left.

To plug it properly, you will have to drill out the existing ragged hole to get a nice clean edge. Then cut a "flat-grained" dowel slightly larger in diameter than the newly drilled hole. Flat-grain means that the grain runs across the face of the dowel rather than along its length, as it normally would. This could be done with a plug cutter (from a woodworking supply store) or you can turn it on a lathe, if you have one. The dowel should be the same species of wood as the body, and the grain should match the pattern of the body. If you put in a piece of a regular dowel, you will obviously not match the flow of the grain, but you might consider it better than the screw that was there before.

Before gluing and driving the dowel, taper it slightly and check it for a snug fit. Make sure the grain is oriented to match the body. Don't drive it in too hard or you might split the body. Cut the dowel off close to the body and flush it off with a chisel or file and then sandpaper. With new wood like the dowel, it's better to stain everything, old wood and new; the match comes out closer. Give the dowel a coat first, and then stain everything with the second coat. You might end up having to darken the dowel to match.

ANIMAL GNAWING AND ROT:

When a wooden tool is left in a barn for years, it becomes a target for animal gnawing. The mice like to chew on the section where the worker's hand left sweaty salt deposits. This malady, and rot (which also comes from years of neglect) are two very tough repairs. Normally the plane is scrapped. It would have to be quite valuable and very ugly from the rot or gnawing, for an owner to try restoration. The repair is almost a surgical procedure. All the bad stuff has to be cut away and new wood fitted in its place. The fit of the new wood is difficult, but remember two things:

1) The fit needs only to be perfect at the *edges*. The inside can be filled with epoxy where it doesn't match closely enough.

2) The new wood should always overflow the spot it's going into. Then when it's all fitted, the repair piece can be sawn off and flushed to match the remaining body.

Sometimes when you start after rot, there is no stopping. It almost seems as if it goes on forever, and the only good wood is the shell of the plane. It pays to poke a needle all over to see how extensive the rot is. You may not want to attempt restoration under any circumstances.

If the rot is under the surface of some reasonably good wood, and not very deep, you might try lifting the good wood away with a razor cut. Then scrape out the rot, and harden it with a deep penetrating hardener (*Wood Hardener*, Minwax, Montvale, NJ). Fill the cavity with epoxy. The good external skin can be put back over the repair and glued down.

I'd give serious thought before starting either of the two repairs above. You might want to merely douse the affected area with a deep penetrating wood hardener and call it quits. It might take a few applications but it is considerably easier and much less risky. Luckily this won't happen very many times on planes valuable enough to consider this restoration.

INLAYS:

I'm sure most everyone has seen those cute little inlays in the sole, just in front of the mouth of bench planes. They were alleged to be repairs, because the sole of the plane wore down and consequently the mouth opened up. It's true that the geometry of the mouth and throat proves that this is technically possible, but let's get real. Almost every one of these planes with the inlays was *not* made by professionals. They are planes made by shipwrights, and others making their own planes, and carvers who want to show their carving skills (with little planemaking skills), home craftsmen etc.

The hardest part of making a bench plane is to have the mouth come through the sole at the right place and with the right size opening. If you haven't taken any instructions, the chances are that you will have the mouth opening far too wide. How to recover? Simple - just put in an inlay, which is not that difficult for a woodworker.

There are planes that were very intricately carved (supposedly in the 17th or 18th century) that are non-functional because of an improper layout. In one case the cutting iron *is made out of wood*, and in another *it doesn't extend out of the mouth*. Some others have the inlay described as "the wonderful skill of the planemaker". Not so. You'll very rarely see a professionally made plane with an inlay. They almost always are the results of mistakes!

I'm sure there are some that actually wore down to the level where an inlay was used, but that's generally the exception, rather than the rule.

ADJUSTED THROAT OPENINGS:

Speaking of non-professional modifications, a common one is an "adjustment" of the opening of the throat of molding planes in order to get a better chip exit. It isn't always done neatly. I like to clean up these modifications without changing their contour or depths to any great degree. After that they look as if they were put in by someone who cared. A file and some sandpaper, or maybe even a chisel, will handle the problem nicely.

BODY REFINISHING:

After all of the restorations above, the body will need to be refinished, so as to blend everything together and simulate as much of the patina as possible. See pages 100 to 107 for the cleaning and refinishing techniques.

WEDGE

There are three different types of wedges in a wooden plane:
1) cutting iron wedge,
2) slitting iron wedge, and
3) fence arm wedge.

The cutting iron wedge is probably the most commonly restored or replaced part of the wooden plane. It's important to copy the proper profile when restoring. These profiles can be found in: *A Guide to the Makers of American Wooden Planes*, Pollak, from Astragal Press, Mendham, N.J.

In addition to the profile, other important factors of the wedge restoration are: the right species (usually beech), proper grain orientation, correct color, and snug fit. It may sound like a lot, but it's like anything else: get a little practice and it turns out well. There are a few tricks, but they are easy.

First, you must get the correct wood, both for species and grain. almost all of the 19th century makers used beech, but the 18th century Americans used both beech and birch. Where the bodies are of less common woods (apple, boxwood, rosewood or ebony) you should use similar woods for the wedges.

I have seen some rosewood plow planes with boxwood arms and a boxwood wedge (a nice two-tone effect). I have also seen some bench planes made by shipwrights out of lignum vitae or ebony to get a better grip by driving the softer beech wood against the hard lignum or ebony. Lignum against lignum, or ebony against ebony doesn't "yield" well when the angle match of the wedge and the wedge-slot in the body is not perfect.

MOLDING PLANE WEDGES:

For a molding plane wedge, cut out a rectangular piece that is slightly thicker than the opening it will fit into. I use a belt sander to bring the thickness almost to size, and finish it off by hand with fine sandpaper (220 grit). Then cut the angle of the wedge by using a cardboard template that fits the opening *when the iron is in place.* Leave plenty of room at both ends. See Fig. 19.

Burnish the edges of the wedge, and drive it home. Correct the angle if it isn't a perfect fit. It should fit tightly in the mortise of the body, all the way down and on all sides. When you are satisfied with the fit, mark the junction of the body and the wedge with a line on the wedge. See Fig. 19.

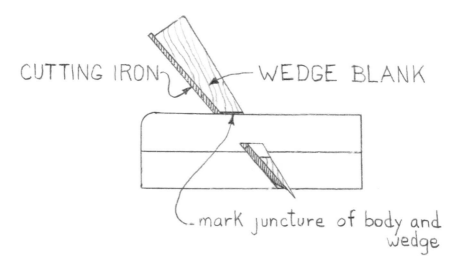

Figure 19

Make a cardboard template of the finial using Pollak's book. If you're good at copying you can draw the finial directly on the wedge blank; but remember it's not a tracing, as the sketches in Pollak's book are not full size. Use the bottom of the sketch in the book to match the horizontal line that you drew on the wedge. See Fig. 20. Cut out the finial (leaving extra wood for final sanding) with a band saw, or the best saw that you can come up with. A coping saw will do.

Some planes have their iron skewed (at a diagonal to the body of the plane, rather than straight across). The wedge

43

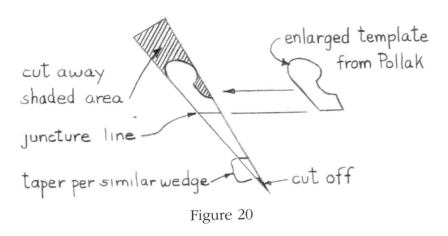

cut away
shaded area

enlarged template
from Pollak

juncture line

taper per similar wedge

cut off

Figure 20

will have to be cut to accommodate this angle. Leave considerably more width than you need, so that if your first try at the angle needs correcting, you will have enough stock to continue.

Complete the wedge by cutting off the tip at the bottom to the correct shape. Check out another similar wedge to get it right. See page 104 for staining and finishing.

BENCH PLANE WEDGES:

Bench plane wedges require chisel work to remove the wood from the chip exit portion of the wedge. If you are not good with a chisel, leave a lot more wood than required, and finish it off with a file and sandpaper. Leave the final thickness of the upper portion of the wedge until last and belt sand it to size, using other wedges of the same maker, or of the period, as a guide.

SLITTING IRON (OR NICKER) WEDGES:

Slitting iron wedges are very similar to molding plane wedges, except they are smaller and take a great angle of taper. The finial should be similar to the cutting iron wedge. Panel and dado planes will be the ones most needing these slitter wedges. There is no difference in procedure in making this wedge than the cutting iron wedge.

FENCE ARM WEDGES:

Fence arm wedges come in two styles:
1) a tapered piece with no finials, and
2) one similar to above but with a finial on the small end of the taper.

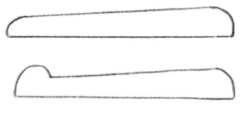

The first style is easier to make, but can fall out of the body when moving the arms, see Fig. 21.

Figure 21

Almost all fence arm wedges are boxwood. If you have the beat-up originals you can tell what wood is right, but if both wedges are missing, boxwood is a good guess. There were some early planes with beech, birch, and even fruitwood arm wedges, but if it's 19th century, you're fairly safe with boxwood.

Cut out a rectangular piece to start and thin it down to a sliding fit through the wedge slot in the body. These slots may be different between the front and rear arms, so make each wedge fit its own slot.

Make a cardboard template for the angle of each slot. (They might be different also.) If you are dealing with just a tapered wedge with no finials, you can cut the taper on as this point. Leave room at each end, and cut the wedge to size after it is marked off in the body with the arms in place.

If there is evidence of the wedge having a finial, draw it on and then cut out the contour of the entire wedge, leaving extra wood in order to finish smoothly. If the taper doesn't match snugly all the way through the body, correct it where needed. You might find that you will have to start over if your first attempt doesn't fit. If you leave more width than required, you might preclude this do-over.

Finish the wedge as described on page 104.

FENCE

There are not many things that can go wrong with the fence that aren't covered in the BODY section. Of course we can go to the extreme of having the fence so far gone, or missing, that only a new one would suffice. I think that goes beyond the scope of this book. However if you feel you have the talent and the right material to go this route, I suggest that you get John Whelan's book *Making Traditional Wooden Planes*, Astragal Press, Mendham, N.J. Remember to check a similar plane for the correct shape.

FENCE ARM:

Of all the repairs on wooden planes, fence arm restorations are the most troublesome. You will have to decide whether the time and/or the risk is worth it. If the answer is yes, here is how:

There are three major kinds of fence arms (excluding some of the more sophisticated bridle types):

1) slide arm with thumbscrew lock,
2) slide arm with wedge lock, and
3) screw arm with nut lock.

Many of the early 18th century plows have fence arms with thumbscrew locks. It would pay to check out the signature in Pollaks' *A Guide to the Makers of American Wooden Planes*. You might have a winner! If you decide to restore, the first thing to do is disassemble the plane.

DISASSEMBLY:

If the thumbscrews are "frozen", do not drench them with oil, any kind of oil. It will only swell the wood. In fact what is needed is the opposite, an effort to dry up and shrink the wood. For this your home oven will do. Set it at 120 degrees and let the plane bake in there for 10 or 15 minutes. Then inspect it for any cracks that might be opening up. If you get any, you might want to forgo any further baking.

If there are no cracks, or if you are daring enough to gamble that the cracks will close up after cool down, *or* if you choose to fill the cracks, then let the plane stay in the oven for at least an hour. If no cracks appear, you can move the temperature up to 150. I have had it up to 220 on stubborn jobs, and saw no problems.

Keep trying to move the thumbscrews during the bake. But if they don't move after 2 hours, take the plane out and let it cool down. They most likely will move then. Moving clockwise and counterclockwise in small degrees, is the best way to break them loose. After they are loose, you can increase the amount of turn.

Some people put the plane in the freezer in an effort to loosen the parts. I've never had as much luck with this as I've had with the drying out technique, but if all else fails — try it.

If *everything* fails, and the thumbscrews are still stuck, you have two choices: forget about taking the arms apart, and do whatever restoring that is needed in the as-is condition, or drill out the thumbscrews and replace them. The latter option is quite drastic and not recommended unless there is so much wrong with the plane that it must come apart if it is to be saved. However, there are times when the thumbscrew is broken off or missing and must be replaced anyhow. So, you ought to know how to make a new one.

If you are lucky, you might find a thumb- screw from a marking gauge that has the right thread pitch (threads per inch). If it's not long enough to reach the arm, you could add a small section of a dowel, by just dropping it into the threaded hole in the body, or gluing it to the end of the thumbscrew. If you can't find the right screw, or even if you find one with the right thread but the wrong wing profile, you might want to carve one from scratch. If there is another thumbscrew that is with the plane and can be removed, you can copy from that one. To carve the threads (it's not likely that you will find the right screwbox) refer to the technique used for carving screw arms on page 51.

Now the arms are loose and ready to come out. This is not always as easy as it should be. If the arms are swollen or warped they will hang up in the hole that they go through in the body, sometimes even after the baking process that was described above. If it is possible, disassemble each arm from the fence to lessen any problem coming from warpage. But, if the arms are also swollen, you will have to sand them down on the exit side of the body. (You can finish sanding the complete arm after it is apart.)

After sanding, hold the body securely in a vise and rap the end of the arm with a mallet. If you get it to move in either direction just sand it until it drives off. Some paraffin or cake wax will help (no oil). Once disassembled, it is an easy job to sand the hole or the arm, or both, until you get a nice slide fit.

Let's suppose that the arm is badly warped and you can't get it disassembled from the body unless you take it apart from its fence, BUT you can't get it apart from the fence due to corrosion or riveting. You can go one of three ways:

1) If the arm is attached to the fence with a machine screw, and it is held by a threaded "diamond" shaped nut recessed in the arm, then you can try penetrating oil and shocking blows. This works almost all the time. If you have to look at the few times when it doesn't work, you are left with the unpleasant task of drilling out the screw and replacing it.

2) If the arm is held to the fence with a riveted rod you could drill it out and make a new rod and rivet it back together. This is quite an invasive repair and if function is not that important your best bet is to leave it alone.

3) If the screw is a wood screw (usually flat-headed and countersunk into the fence) then you have to take a different approach. You can try rapping the screwdriver in the slot of the screw, and you can try ever bigger and bigger screw-drivers. Eventually you might just snap off the head of the screw or break away a part of the slot.

A safer idea is to take a screwdriver that you don't care about and heat it as hot as you can get it with a propane torch (from the hardware store). Then set it into the slot in the screw and let the heat travel through the screw. Keep this up until the screw turns or you see a small whiff of smoke. Keep on working the screw in both directions over and over. It will give up, hopefully before you do. Try not to burn the edge of the hole by leaving the screwdriver in the slot too long. The whiff of smoke mentioned above is your signal that it is time to give it a rest.

You must be prepared for that awful feeling when you are trying to get a screw loose, and it suddenly turns super-easy. You have snapped it! Now you are stuck with drilling out the remains.

This takes a little more concentration than you might think. If you have an end mill that will come down squarely on the broken piece, the problem becomes minimal. But most of us don't have a variety of end mill sizes, so you will have to use a drill.

Flatten the broken end with a punch so that a small drill can start in the center of the screw, without slipping into the wood. You must be prepared for the worst, which is that you can't get the drill to bite directly into the screw. It keeps slipping off into the wood and the hole around the screw is getting bigger and bigger.

Well, if you can't beat 'em, join 'em. Give up trying to drill *into* the screw; drill small holes all around the screw into the wood. There are screw extractors, used in a drill press, that fit down over the screw and cut away a narrow ring of wood (like a hole saw). They work great. If you don't have a set, the crude method above will work almost as well.

Pretty soon you will be able to turn the broken screw with a pair of needlenose pliers. Out it comes, from what looks like the Grand Canyon of all holes. Not to worry. Just drill out the hole so that it is clean all around and plug it with a dowel. If the hole will become hidden, it doesn't matter if you use a piece of a standard dowel. However, if it can be seen and you want to hide the mess you made, it will be necessary to cut the dowel in the flat-grain method described on page 39.

I have occasionally used "easy-outs". These are left-handed tapered spiral shanks that are driven into that hole you drilled in the broken screw. Once locked in, they provide an extension to spin out the screw. If corrosion wasn't part of the problem, these easy-outs would work. But in restoring, corrosion is usually the culprit, and the easy-outs are not effective. I remember snapping off both screws *and* easy-outs, before I became more wary.

STRAIGHTENING WARPED ARMS:

OK, the arm is off the fence and the screw is out and the hole fixed. We are now left with a warped arm. Steam is the best way to bend (or straighten) wood. But it's messy, and not very effective if you don't have the right vessel. So, here's what is second best — and almost as good:

Get a turkey pan, fill it with water a few inches deep and *boil* the arm in it for 15 to 20 minutes. Quickly put it in the vise with spacers wedging the bend out. You should over-straighten it. That means: set it up to be bent back the other way a small amount to compensate for the inevitable spring-back. Leave it in the vise overnight. See Fig.22. Be prepared to have it relieve itself back slightly.

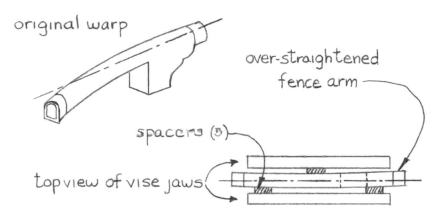

Figure 22

50

If you haven't over-straightened enough, do it again; if you have over-straightened too much (and you should wait a day before deciding this) just boil it again and straighten it back. It's trial and error, until you get the feel of it. Just careful you don't stress the wood and crack the arm. Doing it in steps helps.

END FERRULES:

Some slide arm planes have brass ferrules at both ends of the arm. They are usually loose and sometimes battered. They can be trimmed up with a file and emery paper and glued back in position. Make sure that no dimension of the ferrule sticks out beyond the periphery of the arm or it will jam in the hole in the body.

WEDGE-LOCKED ARMS:

Arms that are wedge locked have just about all the problems described above for thumbscrew locked arms. Making new wedges for these arms is detailed under arm wedges on page 45.

SCREW ARMS:

And now the biggie: screw arms with locking nuts. Most of what's been discussed relative to slide arms pertains also to the screw arms — baking, boiling, removal of screws etc. But the threads on both the arm and the locking nuts present a problem that surpasses anything you have seen to date.

To start with, you stand a risk of a frozen nut on the arm being caused by broken pieces of thread jammed inside the threaded nut. It almost always happens with the large nut rather than the flat one (which is usually called a washer). If this is the case, baking will not help. A bad sign is when the nut turns ever so slightly, but no more, and fine dust is seen to fall from it.

This will probably be a repair so major that it won't be worth the trouble. But if you own the plane and choose to do *something*, rather than leave it the way it is, you can continue

51

to turn the nut back and forth, grinding up thread until it's loose enough to get it off. I can remember once when I actually had to split the nut to get it off.

If the jammed nut is due to swollen wood, you can bake it out as described for the slide arms. It will help considerably to reduce the OD (outside diameter) of the threaded arm and the pitch diameter of the thread. The OD can be done easily with sandpaper, but the pitch diameter of the threads will require a very acute angle file less than 60 degrees (found in a jeweler's file kit). It will have to be done thread by thread. See Fig.23.

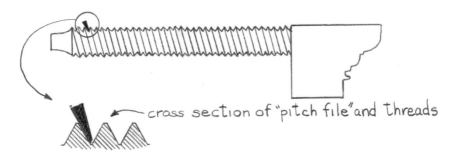

cross section of "pitch file" and threads

Figure 23

While working on the threads, either with sandpaper or a file, have the work over a clean bench. If you chip off a piece of one of the threads, you can glue it back on in a matter of seconds with crazy glue. If the plane has seen some serious drying out, you might get lots more chipping than you would like. You will then have another decision to make: whether to continue to file and sand or leave it as-is.

Let's assume that you were successful in getting everything apart, straightened and working smoothly. But, the arms have their threads chipped slightly in some places, almost to the root in other places, and completely stripped off for an inch or so at the fence end of the arm.

Small chips here and there can be left alone. If they bother you they should be filled with wood filler and then filed and sanded to shape. If you want to strengthen the fills, apply some crazy glue over them after you file them to shape. They will be stronger then you think, particularly if you clean the surface first with acetone. I have never done any damage to the threads that were repaired in this way, no matter how much stress I put against the repaired area.

When a large section of thread is missing, *that* is a tricky repair. However, you do have options:

If you have a lathe, you can turn down the defective section and glue in two semi-circular "C"-sections that were turned and drilled to fit. You will need above average wood-working skills to get both the grain and dimensions to fit perfectly. It's then threaded in a screw box to match the thread on the arm.

I am assuming that the correct screwbox is available. If not, this step will have to be replaced with a more difficult one, which will be explained later. Final trim can be done with a jeweler's file and fine sandpaper.

Some restorers feel it is easier to make an entire threaded portion of the arm and then fit it into the shoulder of the piece that attaches to the fence, Fig.24. I agree that it might be easier, but you are losing more of the original piece. You will have to decide which is more important to you.

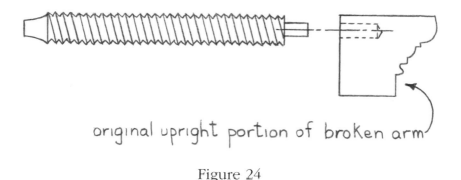

original upright portion of broken arm

Figure 24

Where a screw box is not available to cut the exact thread size needed, you will have to resort to a few complicated techniques, or one simple one that is difficult to do. In either case prepare yourself for frustration and probable failure on the first try.

I'll mention the complicated ones only for completeness. I don't expect too many readers to try them. First you will need a hi-speed grinder that is used like a Dremel tool. In fact a good size Dremel tool will probably work OK. The cutting tool to make the thread is a 60 degree "V" cutter. If you have a lathe that can get you the pitch of the thread, mount the grinder on the tool post and throw the automatic thread feed in at the correct geared position. Unlike a screwbox, you can cut small depths at each pass, and will get a flawless thread if done right. If you don't have a lathe that can get you various thread pitches, then you can use the technique below:

Place the piece to be cut with the grinder or Dremel tool on a rig that is connected to a "master piece" with the exact thread pitch that is desired. The master can be the remains of the defective arm. A stylus inserted into the existing good threads forces the newly cut threads to "follow" and be cut at exactly the same pitch (or spacing). It helps to lightly strap the piece down to prevent it from "jumping."

Clear? No? Look at Fig.25. Clear now? No?

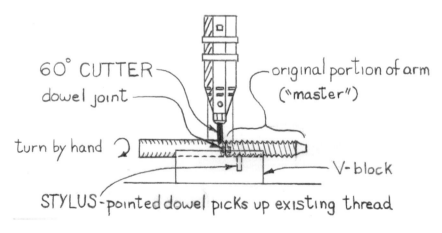

Figure 25

Well, maybe it's best to omit this one and go to the next alternative which is much simpler to understand, but harder to do.

Build up the defective area with layer upon layer of wood filler. Clean each layer with acetone before building the next one. Let them dry hard between applications. File and sand round when there is enough buildup. With a straight edge of cardboard, mark the crest of each thread by laying the straight edge next to the existing good threads, Fig.26(1).

Mark the thread spacing from the cardboard template on the newly built up section at 4 or 5 different places, timing it to start where the existing thread leaves off. Then connect up the marks to form a smooth thread, Fig.26(2).

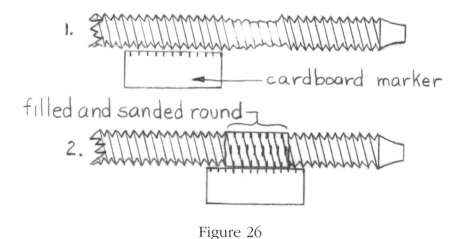

Figure 26

With a small dovetail saw, cut the root of the thread half way between the lines. Then with an Exacto knife, shape in the thread. File and sand it to a smooth form. Any pieces that break off can be glued back immediately with crazy glue. The entire thread can be hardened with a coat of crazy glue when finally shaped. Like I said, it's easy to understand, but not so easy to do.

A common problem with fence arms is the splits in the shoulders (the part that attaches to the fence). Once the arms are disassembled, they can be cleaned and glued under clamping pressure. The joint may be quite visible if some of the edges of the split have chipped away. In this case a wood filler would be in order, with a final smoothing of fine sandpaper and 0000 steelwool. Boxwood (which most arms are made out of) is the hardest wood to match with wood fill. Don't get discouraged if you have to darken the arm a bit to help with the match.

There might be a time when making an entire arm is the only way to put a valuable plane back into "the land of the living". For this I recommend *Making Traditional Wooden Planes*, by John Whelan, (Astragal Press).

FENCE ARM LOCKING NUT:

Unless you have a lathe, making these nuts is not feasible. The flat nuts, called washers, are easier than the larger bulbous nuts, but any lathe hand can copy either easily. The difficult part is the threading, which is made even more touchy in the larger nut, because it is tapped into end grain. There are special taps for end grain, but its not very likely that you will have the exact one. Where very valuable planes are involved, I have had an end grain tap made in a machine shop. I find it easier to tap first and turn on a threaded mandrel last.

Gluing splits in these nuts requires a good cleaning first. Get into the split with an old toothbrush and some alcohol or acetone. You will need quite a bit of clamping pressure to close up some of these cracks, and might have to use the "gorilla" glues mentioned on page 36.

After the split is closed, it is possible that the nut no longer turns easily on the arm. As such, you will have to clean out some threads in the nut, and maybe on the arm too. External threads on the arm are not tough; just follow the advice on page 51.

It is not that easy with internal threads such as in the nuts. Here you will need a boring tool (machinist's) or a dentist's hook tool, Fig.27. The tools are used by hand, scraping the internal thread.

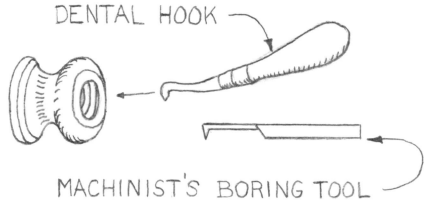

DENTAL HOOK

MACHINIST'S BORING TOOL

Figure 27

Filing the internal diameter of the thread, the smallest diameter of the female thread, will greatly help. However, you must use a fine round file or you will chip the threads. Sandpaper wrapped around a rat-tail file almost the size of the hole is the safest way to handle this operation.

HANDLE:

If the handle of a plane is missing, or if it needs to be replaced entirely, I once again suggest *Making Traditional Wooden Planes* by John Whelan. However, what is usually the case is:

1) The handle is split and needs to be re-glued or,

2) the tip of the handle is broken off and needs to be replaced.

A split handle should be treated much the same as a split fence arm, i.e. clean it with alcohol or acetone and glue it under clamping pressure. If some of the edges of the split have broken away, they should be filled with wood filler, and then sanded and refinished as per page 105.

A broken-off tip is another problem. This takes some creative restoration. In almost all cases the broken-off part is gone, and a new tip has to be made. I have seen some pretty horrible repairs of this sort. Here's how to do it right:

Get a piece of wood of the same species and the same grain flow. It's much easier to see the grain in the cross section. Grain orientation is more important than you think. When the grain matches, stain will take care of almost everything else (assuming the joint is made tight). Although you might need a number of pieces to find a good grain match, it's worth it when you are done. A good match and a tight joint is what makes the job look professional.

To get a tight joint, you will first have to cut off the broken tip on the grain line, see Fig.28. Sand this area flat on the disk portion of a stationary belt sander, or a hand block — taking care not to roll the edges, *not even the slightest bit.* You may not believe how easy it is to roll the edge, even with what you think is the utmost care. I have found that part of the problem can be eliminated by taping the sandpaper to a flat plate and bearing down equally on all areas of the part being sanded. It works better than moving the sandpaper over the part.

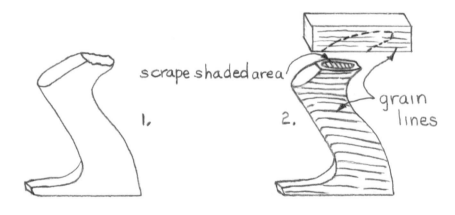

Figure 28

Orient the wood that is going to be the new tip so that the grain matches the handle. Sand the mating surface flat as you did above. Then with an Exacto knife, scrape the center of the flattened surface *on the handle* so that only an outer ring of that surface will touch the mating area of the new tip. If you have scraped too deeply, re-sand the surface with the block or on the belt. Do not use power at this stage. The mating contact surface should not be any more than a $\frac{1}{8}$" wide ring, no higher than a sheet of paper from the scraped surface. Removing any high spots in the center of the joint allows a tighter fit at the edges. See Fig.28(2).

When clamping during gluing, it helps to put a dowel behind the added piece. It will make up for any non-parallel surfaces, and allow you to increase clamping pressure without squeezing the joint open. See Fig.29.

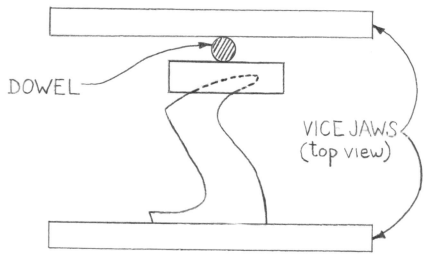

Figure 29

After gluing, cut the new piece down to *almost* the thickness of the existing handle. A band saw is easiest, but a back saw will work also. Pencil on the extended tip of the handle and cut it out on the band saw or a coping saw. If you have a flexible shaft router with a sanding head, this is a per- fect place for it. If you don't, you'll have to bull it through with files and sandpaper. Leave more wood in the rough than you think you'll need. You will end up needing every bit of it, par- ticularly on your first try.

Sand down the entire handle with fine sandpaper, then 0000 steelwool and then a burnishing rod. Finish per page 104.

You will find that the darker woods will hide more mistakes than the lighter ones. Boxwood is almost unforgiving, but rosewood allows many slight errors to go almost undetected.

CUTTING IRON:

Remember what was said in the Introduction of this book: **Antique tools should be in the same condition today as they were a hundred or more years ago in the hands of a prideful worker**. If you prefer to have your tools follow this adage, then the cutting irons must have a proper edge. Some people make replacement blades from low carbon steel because it can be filed into shape instead of the more difficult grinding that is required of steel that is hardened. The cutting edges of these "look alikes" are not what any worker would be content with, prideful or not.

The cutting irons for yesteryear's planes were made of wrought iron with a thin layer of good steel layed-on the iron by hammer forging. The line of demarcation can easily be seen on the blade's underside, as the steel is smoother and lighter in color than the iron. These are the blades that should be used for replacement.

I previously suggested that you buy beat-up axes so that you can use the handles as replacements. It is the same with beat-up planes. When the wood in the plane is near total destruction, the cutting iron might be the only thing left of value. I have boxes of irons that I have taken from worthless planes, and have been able to re-grind them to fit really nice planes. It is not that hard.

The equipment needed is a bench grinder, preferably dual ended, $1/2$ horsepower, 3450 RPM. (You probably could get away with a $1/3$ H.P., and even 1725 RPM). Mount a $3/4$" wheel on one end and a wheel that's tapered down to $1/8$" on the other end. These two wheels should allow you to grind just about any iron. The surfaces of the wheels can be dressed to any profile with a star dresser or a diamond dresser. I dress the $3/4$" wheel with a flat grinding surface, and the $1/8$" wheel with a half-round one. I've never needed anything else, even though there were times when I had to dress the $\frac{1}{8}$" wheel down to a smaller radius.

MOLDING PLANE CUTTING IRONS:

For molding plane irons, grind the profile completely off the replacement blade, unless it is close enough to merely require a trimming up. Once the blade is blanked, set it into the plane in its normal position. Draw on the profile of the sole with a marking pen. Grind it square to the blade first; then taper the lower side of the blade to provide the cutting edge. You will have to keep checking as you go, to be assured that you have equal edge protrusion throughout the full profile.

Keep the blade cool by frequent water dips. Do not allow any discoloration. If you do, you will compromise the hardness and temper that is already there. Hone the profile with flat stones and round, tapered stones.

I like to clean off any rust or oxidation from the blade with a wire wheel, concentrating on not hitting the edge. You may wish to "age" the newly ground surfaces with some gun bluing. See page 110. Whether you do or not, always oil the blade before putting it back in the plane

NICKER IRONS:

Nicker blades were usually made from all steel. If you don't have any real spare parts, they can be made from small files. If you want to utilize 20th century stuff, buy a piece of oil-hardening tool steel, which can be cut with a hacksaw and filed. For the purpose that you are going to use it (slitting), it is probably hard enough as-is, but if you choose, you can harden it with a home style heat treatment:

Heat it up to cherry red with your propane torch, quench immediately in oil, clean off the oxidation, and "draw it back" to a proper temper with a torch until it turns a straw color. Even if it's not perfectly hardened, it will be good enough for a nicker blade. A word of caution: practice on a scrap piece first. If you overheat beyond the straw color, you will not get exactly what you want, and may have to do it over.

BENCH PLANE IRONS:

Bench plane irons are so plentiful that I have never had to make any. If you don't have a large supply, you may have to grind the blade down in width to exactly fit your plane. This can be done on a bench grinder first and a belt sander to finish off. Take equal amounts off both sides.

If the cutting edge of the iron is merely dull it can be sharpened with a stone, but if it is abused or ragged you will have to use a belt sander or grinder. Be sure to cool the blade by dipping it into water every 4 or 5 seconds of grind. When you are finally grinding the fine edge (to get the burr that indicates that you have finished), go lightly on the pressure in order not to burn the steel. If you want to play safe, use a stone on the final passes to produce the burr.

OTHER PARTS (FOR WOODEN PLANES):

There are a few other parts that you might find require some attention, if you are doing a full restoration.

When cleaning a plane with a screwed-on skate (plow or match planes), it always helps to take out the screws and remove the skate from the body. In this way you can clean the skate easier, particularly if you choose to use a fine wire wheel to finish it off.

The heads of the screws can also be cleaned of rust easier if they are disassembled. If the screws are frozen, you might want to clean the skate in-place, rather than attempting the many screw removal methods described on page 48. But if you do disassemble, keep the screws in the order that they were removed. I use a block of wood with lined-up holes drilled for the screws. This way, they will be returned to the skate exactly as they were, and will seat properly.

The metal depth stops for plow planes are easily jammed to the point that they are very tough to move, and sometimes won't move at all. Remove the screws from the depth stop plate. You might find that the slots in these screws are just not deep enough to get a good grip. Use your Exacto knife or a narrow graver's tool to "chisel" the slots deeper. Once the screws are out, the slots can be properly deepened with a small hacksaw.

Unscrew the wing screw completely out of the body. This will give you a clear shot to drive the depth stop out of its bound-up position. Once out, you can file the stop or the mortise, or both, until you get a snug running fit.

There is another problem that you might encounter with this stop: the thumbscrew floats up and down with a lot of slop. This is due to the collar (under the plate) breaking loose from the threaded stud attached to the thumbscrew. This collar is usually brass, soldered or pinned to the threaded stud. If either of these fastening methods are broken, you will get slop in the thumbscrew. Resolder or repin, whichever is the easiest for you. See Fig.30.

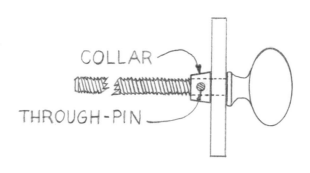

Figure 30

There are a few specialty planes that have parts that are not described here. Eventually you will be able to handle these parts similar to the way described in previous pages. The details will be different, but the techniques will be the same. All that is required is some inherent skills in working with tools, practice and much patience

WOOD-BOTTOMED PLANES

There are 4 major sub-assemblies on wood-bottomed planes that are not on wooden planes:

1) cast iron base and screws,

2) cast iron frog with adjusting stud and brass adjusting nut (or nuts) and screws,

3) cast iron cap with brass locking nut, or toggle lock with hold-down screw, and

4) wood front knob and screw.

To restore a wood-bottomed plane properly, it must first be disassembled. Usually, there is no corroded screw problem (that is prevalent on older all-wood planes). But, with all the cast iron parts, there probably will be more rust.

JAPANNING:

If the japanning that coats the cast iron is just chipped here and there, it can be enhanced with an artist's brush and japan from an art store.

When the original japanning is almost completely gone, the rust and whatever is left of the japanning should be cleaned off with a small scraper (a screwdriver or dull chisel will do). Finish the removal with emery paper, and a wire brush, or a wire wheel if it will fit into the space to be cleaned.

At this point the part can be re-japanned. You can use the stuff from the art store, or the real japanning (which is a tar base product that was used by Stanley). It was being sold by a few tool dealers. Inquire around at some of the club meetings to see if it is still available.

Sherwin-Williams Co. puts out a High Heat Black #1614 (*KRYLON*), which I consider a good simulation of the original japanning. It can be sprayed on, coat after coat, with only 5 minutes between coats. It can be baked at 225 to 250 degrees afterward. If you can build up enough coats, you will *come close* to putting the plane in the same condition that it was in when it was on the bench of a prideful worker around 100 years ago.

Look closely at what the original japanning covered. Any machined area was probably machined *after* japanning, and therefore should show bare metal. It may be hard to distinguish these bare areas, because most of the time they are dark with oxidation and look like they were japanned. The seat of the frog, the lateral adjustment lever, and the head of screws are areas that more than likely did not get japanned. Screws will not be there when you spray, but the other areas will need to be masked off.

If the finished spray is not shiny enough, you can apply some wax or French polish, see page 106. If it comes out too shiny, you can dull it down with some very light rubbing with 0000 steelwool. Usually, the spray mentioned above (which is a semi-gloss) comes out close to the original finish. I have rarely had to adjust it. Simulated japanning provokes a very negative response from some collectors. When the part has high gloss black paint dripping from everywhere, who could blame them? So do it right.

CLEANING:

The brass parts can be cleaned with a *very* fine brass wire wheel or 0000 steelwool and then polished if you choose, see page 107. Steel or iron parts such as studs, screws, blades etc. are cleaned the same no matter what style of plane they came from: wire wheel (emery paper first if the rust is heavy), then a light coat of machine oil. Wood knobs and wood handles are cleaned and stained if needed per page 100.

HANDLE FIT:

The handle of any wood-bottomed plane is attached to its base by means of a threaded stud or screw that goes entirely through the handle. But, if the handle remains loose no matter how much you tighten it, the thread of the screw or of the stud is most likely bottoming in the threaded hole in the base casting. This can be caused by an overly long *replacement* stud or a shrinkage of the handle. In either case, it's easy to merely grind off, or file off, the end of the threaded stud until the handle tightens properly.

REPAIRING THE HANDLE TIP:

If you are repairing the tip of the handle on a wood-bottomed plane, you have an additional thing to consider: the hole through the handle. This hole has a counterbore or a countersink at the top of the handle to accommodate the brass nut or the screw head that tightens the handle to the body. If the repair is at the very tip of the handle "spur", it will not reach this hole, and you can repair the handle the same as you would for an all-wood plane. See page 57.

But, if the repair is large enough to go into or beyond the stud hole and counterbore, you will have to take precautionary measures to assure proper angular alignment of the hole, and also that you keep from chipping the edge of the counterbore.

It will prove easier in the long run to prevent the juncture line of the repair from running *into* the counterbore. When this happens you are left with a "half-hole" to drill out. Even with a Forstner bit or a milling cutter, this is tricky. It is better to make the repair with the juncture line beyond the counterbore, Fig.31.

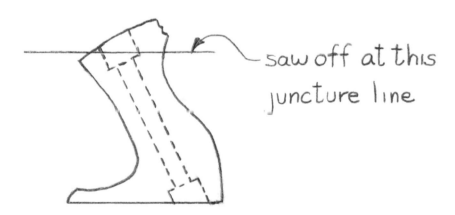

saw off at this juncture line

Figure 31

If you do have to cover up the hole with the added tip, drill the hole through the tip from the *bottom* of the existing hole in the handle, Fig.32. This will maintain the angle and position near perfect. If you are going to use a machinist's drill bit it will usually require a special length bit, as the standard drills are too short.

Cut the profile of the tip *after* drilling, making sure that it is slightly heavier than need be so that any chipping that may happen later can be sanded out. See Fig 32.

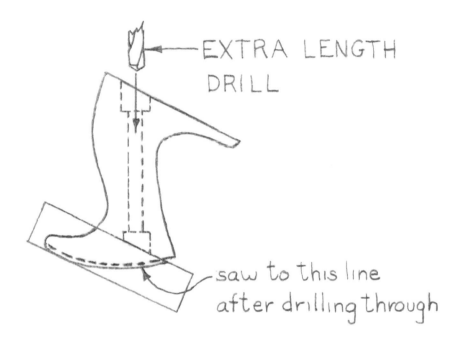

EXTRA LENGTH
DRILL

saw to this line
after drilling through

Figure 32

After drilling the stud hole, reposition the handle in the vise: top side up with the bit in the hole. Clamp the vise to the table, and remove the stud hole drill bit. Then drill the counterbore to full depth, allowing for the additional wood that you left. See Fig.33.

Sand the top of the new piece to its final size, and check to see if the counterbore is deep enough. If not, it can be repositioned as above and drilled deeper. Don't start the

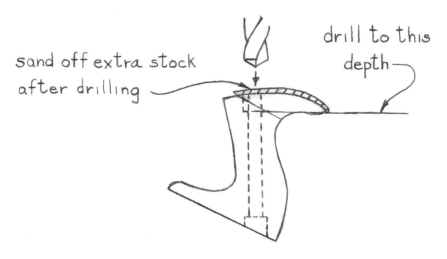

sand off extra stock
after drilling

drill to this
depth

Figure 33

drill until it is near the bottom of the counterbore. This will prevent any chipping if you haven't set the angle or the position perfectly. If you have made the counterbore a little too deep, you can sand a corresponding amount off the top of the handle. If there is too much sanding needed, put a washer at the bottom of the counterbore.

CAST IRON CHIPS AND CRACKS:

Chips and cracks in the cast iron can be fixed, if so desired. Sometimes the base casting falls apart when disassembled because it's been cracked clean through. The broken area can be cleaned with alcohol or acetone and glued back together with the *gel-type* crazy glue (*KRAZY GLUE* by Borden Co.). If the casting is only cracked partially, you will have to use the *regular* crazy glue that will run into the crack.

After a few minutes, emery paper the area to blend the iron dust and the glue together in order to fill any tiny chipped edges. Any larger chips can be filled (a layer at a time) with any two-part 5 minute epoxy, and sanded smooth after drying. If the crack is in a japanned area, re-japan it after it is filled, but don't bake it. The epoxy might not be able to take the heat.

METAL PLANES

The significant difference between the all- metal plane and the wood-bottomed plane is the base casting. On the all-metal plane the casting includes the sole, while on the wood-bottomed plane the casting is mounted to a wooden sole. The sides of the casting in the metal plane are almost always machined square and smooth to the sole, whether the sole is corrugated or not.

There are some planes that have *steel* soles and some even with steel sides. For the purpose of cleaning, steel and cast iron will be treated in the same way.

The cleaning and re-japanning is done in the manner described previously on page 64, with the obvious exception that the machined sides will have to be worked over with emery paper and a wire wheel to get rid of the rust. They will take no coating. If there is deep pitting on either the sides or the sole, you will have to resort to a belt sander if you wish it removed.

A better way is with a surface grinder, but that is outside of the tooling covered in this book. I once bought a collection from a man who owned a large machine shop. For whatever reason, he had every plane stripped of japan, painted with some kind of gloss enamel and then rough surface ground, leaving longitudinal tool marks. It took me longer to scrape off the enamel, re-japan, and polish out the tool marks than if he would have left the planes completely as found. Be careful that you don't overdo this restoration business.

PLATING:

With the later model metal planes, you will run into a surface coating that was not used on earlier planes, namely: nickel plate. Because plating adherence on cast iron was not always easy, the original surface was first "struck" (lightly plated) with copper, and *then* nickel-plated. In an effort to clean up the nickel, you could expose a pink cast of copper, particularly if you get a little over-exuberant with the wire wheel or emery paper. It's an unnatural look and should be avoided.

One way is to just leave it alone, but I find that hard to do when almost all the nickel is gone and rust prevails. In this case you should take it *all* off: rust, nickel and copper, and polish the bare casting with a fine grade wire wheel. It won't look exactly like the nickel, but it will certainly be better than rust.

If only a few areas of the nickel plate have flaked, or are flaking, you can elect to "feather off" just those spots with fine emery paper. They usually occur where the iron surface is the smoothest because that's where the adhesion is the worst. Of course you could play it safe and dab some French polish over the flakes to keep them from coming off. It depends upon degree, and personal preference.

As long as we are on plating, let's discuss plated screws — the kind that you get from the hardware store and want to use as replacements. I don't think I have to mention that Phillip's head or other modern heads are a no-no. However, I have seen many replaced screws with the zinc plate sticking out like a sore thumb.

If you can't buy unplated screws from the hardware store, then buy them from flea markets or house sales even if they are rusted. Rust is easier to get off than zinc plate, and a little of it burnished-in gives character.

If you have to get a certain size that you can find no where else except ones that are zinc-plated, then burn off the plate with your propane torch. Make sure that you have proper ventilation, particularly if the plating is cadmium (which you might find on the earlier plated screws).

You can polish them on the wire wheel after the plating is removed. If the sooty finish that you get fits the rest of the plane, wipe them off and forget about the polishing.

REPLACEMENT PARTS:

You should try to keep a box of spare parts that you can take from otherwise scrap planes. Just throw them in a box. It's like a treasure hunt every time you need one of these parts. You will have to know your models fairly well if you intend to cannibalize in this manner, particularly if the plane has value. If you are just trying to get a common plane functional so that you can use it, the correct part is obviously not as important. It's your decision.

One part that you should buy, any time the price is right, is the blade or iron. If you can get them in sets, so much the better. Some sets today are worth as much as the plane. Blades are easy to clean on the wire wheel, and if they need sharpening, usually a stone will do it.

It's surprising how many planes are missing a blade. Besides from being lost in the normal way, they are frequently stolen from unattended booths in co-op type shops. The culprit rationalizes that the dealer can easily replace the blade. The truth is (and I'm sure that the crook knows it) that a missing rare blade seriously detracts from the value of the plane

HANDLE REPAIRS:

Handles on most American metal planes are similar to those on wood-bottomed planes, and the repairs are the same. However, the classic English metal planes have their wooden handles fit into the wood fill of the casting, or are integral to the fill piece. There is no stud through the handle. They are repaired in the same manner as the handles on all-wood planes.

CAST IRON CHIPS AND CRACKS:

The repairs are identical to those done on wood-bottomed planes. See page 68.

MEASURING TOOLS

RULES

Rules are simple tools, but difficult to restore effectively. That's because: 1) although some warpage can be corrected, the last bit is hard to get, and that is enough for a downgrading, 2) the hinge joint is delicate and does not respond well to any straightening that might be needed to take warp out of the rule, 3) cracks cannot be filled and sanded off smoothly as the markings will be removed, and 4) when cleaning you can't rub too hard or you will again remove the markings. Sounds like you can't get there from here! But there are some things that you can do.

CLEANING:

Just plain dirt and grime can be removed with a light detergent (*Fantastik* or the like) and a cloth. Be careful that you do not remove the markings also. The brass ends and the hinges can be polished lightly with a brass polish or with some 0000 steelwool. Many collectors frown upon brilliant brass, particularly on rules. A rule should look like it was used every day, and that would preclude a brilliant shine.

An easy to use product is *NEVR-DULL*,(George Basch Co. Freeport, N.Y.). It is an impregnated wadding that can be controlled in small pieces. You might want to mask off the wood to prevent losing any finish that might still be there.

The amount of finish still remaining on the rule is going to present you with another one of your restoration decisions. Is there enough decent finish left to leave it the way it is, with just a light cleanup, or is there so little finish left that it would be better to completely refinish it?

If your decision is to refinish, you will first have to remove whatever remains of the old finish. If it is really grungy, you can use a small amount of stripper with some 0000 steelwool. Use a swiping motion, watching carefully that you are not removing markings. The last bit of finish can be taken off with dry steelwool.

Refinish with the *dark* wax and then French polish. They will darken the markings, preserve the wood and coat the brass to keep it from tarnishing. See page 106 for French polishing.

IVORY RULES:

If the rule is ivory and has German silver trim, you will have to be much more careful, as the markings come off easier and German silver will show up almost any scratch. German silver is an alloy of copper and zinc with an addition of nickel, which gives it a silvery appearance.

If there is a crack in the ivory, it is almost impossible to make it disappear. If it is not filled with dark grime, you can try filling it with ivory dust (from sanding scrap pieces of ivory, such as piano keys etc.) mixed with one of the crazy glues. You will have to be quick to get it off the lines and numbers, but it will "dampen" the unsightliness of the crack.

ENHANCING THE MARKINGS:

If you inadvertently take off some of the markings, or they are very faint to start with, you have a few options. Coat the cleaned surface with French polish (or any sealer) and rub into what's left of the markings a mixture of lampblack and linseed or tung oil. You will have to experiment with the mixture to get it as black as possible and not too runny. I let it dry for 5 or 10 minutes and then wipe it off with a rag on a flat block.

If this doesn't do it, and you feel both brave and talented, scratch the markings deeper with a hardened needle-point scribe. You will probably have to use a magnifier head piece to stay within the original lines. It will take some practice. Then brush the lampblack into the newly engraved lines and wipe it off as detailed above.

If the rule is ivory, it will take real talent and much more time than most people are willing to spend. And more important is the risk of making a mess out of an otherwise acceptable rule. If you have the time and the skill, it *can* be done. That's how rules were originally marked before stamping machines automated the process.

I have to admit that I have never done an *entire* rule this way. Too risky, as I'm bound to foul it up somewhere on those many lines and numbers. Once the lampblack ordeal is over, you can put another coating of French polish over everything to seal it all.

ALIGNMENT PINS:

The alignment or closing pins that keep the folds or sections of the rule in line with each other, are sometimes missing. They usually are of brass and between .040" and .048" in diameter. This is a hard size to buy at any of the factory supply houses. If you cannot find the right size, you can skimp with a .030" diameter pin.

Some rule collectors aren't concerned about these pins being missing. The face pins are gone a good percentage of the time anyway, as they were removed by the users so as to have the rule lay flat on that side.

Put a slight point on the end to be pushed into the rule and use a tiny dab of crazy glue. Cut them off to about $\frac{3}{32}$" stickout for the ones that mate edge to edge, and a little less for the ones that mate face to face. File a tiny rounded chamfer on the ends that were cut off to allow a smooth entry into the mating hole in the rule. See Fig.34.

LOOSENING THE SLIDING BAR:

One fix that shows good results is when the sliding L-bar on caliper rules is stuck in its groove. In order to make it functional, you must get the bar to move easily. Hold the rule in the vise with the bar above the jaws of the vise. Tap the bar with a piece of hardwood until you can get it out. Once disassembled from the body of the rule, you can clean both the sliding bar and the groove.

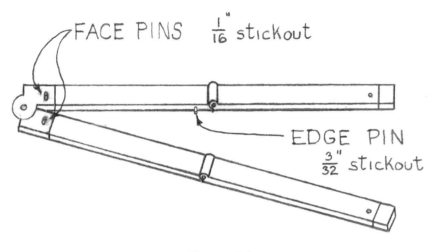

FACE PINS $\frac{1}{16}$" stickout

EDGE PIN
$\frac{3}{32}$" stickout

Figure 34

If it is still bound up after cleaning, you will have to remove material from the slide or the groove, or both. Be careful that you don't disfigure the dovetail joint that these parts use to mate with each other.

There are some rules that have a straight slide without an "L" on the end. These usually have a "fingernail" notch on either end of the slide to help get it started. If the slide is stuck, you can use this notch to position the hardwood block for tapping.

Once disassembled, the slide and the groove should be cleaned and freed up so that it will move smoothly under hand pressure but not by gravity.

BINDINGS:

These are thin flat pieces of German silver or brass pinned to the edges of the more premium rules. A pin or two might be missing causing the binding to separate from the rule. As almost all of these pins are steel (at least on the Stanley rules), you can usually use a small brad to fix the problem.

If the original pin is broken off and still in the rule, you will find it too troublesome to drill out. Just glue the binding down with crazy glue. If you can get a new pin in, cut it off flush and file it smooth. The same repair would apply for pins missing in end plates or hinges. (Some of the larger end plates have brass pins.)

LEVEL VIALS:

Level vials are found in combination rules, and at times are dry or missing altogether. Use the replacement technique described on page 80. Very small vials are hard to get, and most often have to be taken from a lesser piece.

PLUMB BOBS

Plumb bobs are usually of brass, and mostly made of three pieces: 1) the screw-on top, which the string goes through, 2) the body, and 3) the steel screw-on tip. There are some single-piece bobs (usually cast iron), ones with reversible tips, and complicated bobs that have external or internal reels for the string. The latter type takes mechanical ability to disassemble, free up the parts to function, and reassemble. If you don't feel up to it, take it to someone who does — or leave it alone.

The screw-on top can usually be loosened with penetrating oil and some hits with a wooden block. If you can get a good grip on the body in the wooden jaws of a vise, and protect the top from the jaws of a pair of vise grips, you will almost always break it loose.

The steel tip is another matter. In most cases it would be replaced if the bob fell and the tip was damaged. However, I think they were rarely replaced, and through time became almost permanently affixed to the body. Unless there is a hole through the tip to put a rod in (to help spin it off), I would not try to remove a frozen tip.

Some of the longer steel bobs were filled with mercury. Because of the high toxicity of mercury, be careful how you disassemble any bob that feels heavier than it looks.

If the external reel is stuck, see if the flanges of the reel are bent and interfering with its ability to spin. If you find them bent, straighten them out with a pair of needlenose pliers. If not, some penetrating oil and a back and forth turning usually loosens it up.

CLEANING:

Where the plumb bob is almost black with oxidation, it would be correct to polish it to some degree. I usually polish the surfaces that are easy to get at, and leave the others with a little oxidation. It gives it a better natural look, as opposed to the entire bob being dipped in some brass cleaner.

There are some collectors who prefer to remove the nicks, and others that say the nicks give character. Take your pick. A good going over with varying grits of emery paper will take out the little nicks. I rarely try to remove the deeper ones.

A WORD OF CAUTION:

There are two styles of plumb bobs that for lack of a better description I will call "imitations". Originally they were not made to cheat anyone, at least it wouldn't appear so. However, recently more of these imitations have come into the marketplace. Whether for profit or to show off skills is hard to say.

I am including them in this book because one of the advantages the reader will carry away with him after digesting these pages is how to tell when a part has been restored or when a complete tool has been recently made. It may not happen at the first reading, but if you try some of the techniques described, you will eventually see the subtleties that will enable you to pick out restorations and imitations. (I make a serious distinction between the two).

The first style is the "novelty" plumb bob. These were crafted from almost any conceivable tapered container that was available. Some of the nicer ones were made from tea strainers and filled with lead or any other weighty material. I like them. I even have a few in my collection. But I call them what they are: imitations.

The second type is a little more dangerous. They are the ivory ones. Now I don't see much wrong with making a gorgeous presentation bob out of ivory. Many were made just to show off the skill of the craftsman. It's hard for me to believe they were actually used as plumb bobs. Many don't even have metal tips. And they are not very heavy. But they sure look good.

Most all of the more recent imitations were made from pool balls. You are now talking about a size restriction, as most of these early ivory billiard balls are around $2\frac{1}{4}$" in diameter. The only difference that I can point to between a 19th century imitation and a 20th century one is motive. I think the recent ones are more suspect to being fraudulent unless called *contemporary*.

LEVELS

Levels can show the virtues of restoration more than any other tool. Visualize a weather-beaten level that is nicked up, has tarnished brass and broken vials. It's not only ugly but non-functional. In a couple of hours, you can have it showing beautiful grain, shining brass and perfectly level vials. If you put it up for display, you'd get oohs and ahhhs. That's one of the rewards of restoring.

WOODEN SPIRIT LEVEL:

These are the most common of the levels, so common that some aren't worth the time to fix. I hate to admit it, but I buy old levels in the flea markets to get the vials. These are usually mason levels that have 5 or 6 vials and look like something that the cat wouldn't even bother to drag in. They are not very old either; just old enough to have clear liquid in their vials, rather than the yellow or green stuff that is no good for replacements.

I twitch a little when the band saw cuts them into small pieces, so that the vials can be more easily removed. But that's life. After the scrap pieces are in the trash can, I turn around and forget all about what I just did.

So let's assume that the level we are going to restore is worth it. The wood is cherry or mahogany, or if we are really lucky — rosewood. There is plenty of brass — top plate, nicely profiled side plates, thick end plates, and best of all, edge bindings. And to top it off, it has a good signature with patent dates.

It's in such bad shape that no one picked it up to see the price. If I bought this winner, I would be salivating all the way home in anticipation of the before and after magic that was about to be performed.

I've been asked why I don't take before and after photographs of the better restorations. Maybe I'm just too lazy, but I never felt that the camera could show the real difference. Yes, it *looks* better after the restoration, but that is not the most important difference. There is a *feeling* about a well restored piece that only the restorer experiences. It helps make up for the times when things break or you hit your thumb etc. etc.

I usually disassemble all the plates (but not the edge bindings), before I clean the wood. I mark the plates with their respective places, and I keep the screws in a board with holes, in their respective places. At times, you will find a stripped screw or two in the top plate that keeps turning but does not come out. After removing all of the other screws, gently pry the plate up with a screwdriver to get the stripped screw out. A series of various size screw drivers is a must for any restorer. I think I have at least 8 that I match to the screw.

When reassembling the plate, break off a toothpick in the hole that held the stripped screw. This will tighten it up. If not, break off another piece. Make sure that any new screw matches the existing ones, in size, shape and material.

CLEANING, SANDING AND STAINING:

Most of the work is going to be done on the wood. If the varnish is gone and the wood is badly nicked and scratched, just stripping it won't be good enough. You will

79

have to sand it down. Yes, I said *sand it.* Sanding has always been looked at on the same level as spitting tobacco juice in church. I don't really know why, but I suspect it was because the person sanding left a worse mess than what was there originally. Like many plumbers who are called to fix things that the husband started to fix, I have been asked to fix a few home projects also. Some have been involved with sanding, and they were truly a mess. So let's sand the right way:

If you have some deep rips in the wood, do not try to sand them out. They should be filled. Sanding is only for shallow surface problems. Number 80 grit is about as heavy as you should go, sequencing down to 120 grit then 220 grit. I don't use a belt sander on levels because there is a chance of taking off too much wood. You can get the job done with a hand sand block. And, if you can't get the plates off, or if the level is edge bound, it forces you to hand sand anyway. When you have filled all the holes and cracks with wood filler, you can finish sanding the entire level. Then rub it with steelwool and a burnishing rod to close up the grain.

Next is the staining of the wood. Don't stain mahogany, or rosewood too red. Some of the cherry levels were overly stained red at the factory, but they are mostly the later, less expensive models. Test the stain on a similar piece of wood first. When you have it the way you want it, rub it into the finished surfaces. The final coating will be put on after all the parts are cleaned and assembled. See page 105.

Clean the brass, including the screws, on the rag wheel, using tripoli or rouge, see page 108. If the corrosion is heavy, you might want to use a fine emery paper first, before using the rag wheel.

VIAL REPLACEMENT:

And now, the tough one — replacement of the vial. If the vial had a small break, the fluid has long since leaked out. You will have to dig the plaster-of-paris away from what's left of the vial. Don't take all the plaster out as it will make a base for the new vial.

If the vial is adjustable, you will have to remove two more screws to get the vial assembly out. Pick a new vial that fits in length, diameter and arc. Even though the arc of the vial is meaningless if the piece is to be just kept in a collection, it should be right *if* you have a selection of vials to pick from.

The rule is that the smaller the radius of the arc (which gives a higher arch to the vial) the slower the air bubble will move in the vial. These slow bubbles are more suitable for carpentry, while the flatter vials with faster bubbles are correct for machinists. Usually, you can be happy that you have a vial even close to the original.

Some vials have one centering line, some two, and an occasional early one — none. Most early vials have thin lines; the later ones are thicker. Try to match the replacement vial to the one being removed. As I mentioned before, whatever you do, don't use a vial with colored fluid. One last caveat: make sure the arch of the vial is pointing up if it is the horizontal leveling vial, and pointing to the nearest end of the level if it is the vertical or plumb leveling vial. See Fig.35.

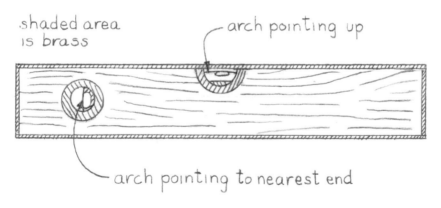

Figure 35

Getting out the plumb leveling vial is a little tougher. The adjustable vials are covered with a screwed on plate. Remove this and pull out the brass vial cover with the vial. Needlenose pliers will do it. Some of the plumb vial assemblies are attached to the plate, and come out with the plate. Many of the earlier levels have no plates, but just a round cover the size of a penny. You'll have to do a lot of digging with this type, but the vial is broken anyway, so you can't do too much more damage.

If you don't want to use plaster-of-paris or its equivalent, try spackling paste. It takes a while to dry (overnight) but it's easier to work with.

LEVELING THE REPLACEMENT VIAL:

The toughest part in getting the replaced vial back in position is in making sure it's level or plumb. There are different ways to get the vials to be positioned properly:

1) Horizontal vial

Fill your bathtub or any large vessel with a few inches of water. Get a board that is flat and true and about the length of the level. Float the board in the bathtub and place the level on the board. If the vial that you have temporarily leveled in the center cavity of the level shows level, you can let the paste (or whatever you are using) dry. If it's not level, change the position of the vial until it is.

You can also level the horizontal vial by putting the level on a good flat surface (such as the table on your band saw) and adjust it until it reads exactly the same after flipping it end for end. This method is a little less accurate but considerably easier.

2) Vertical vial (plumb vial)

Hang a plumb bob along any upright column. If it is truly vertical according to the bob, use it to test the vertical vial in your level. If the column is slightly off, look for a better one. If there isn't any column that is perfectly true, tape a board vertically onto any column and match it dead true to the string of the bob. Test the level against this board.

I have a "master level" that I test this way every so often. I use it to test all other restored levels, so I don't have to go through this rigmarole every time I replace a vial.

I don't trust any level as a master just because it *looks* right, even brand new ones. I had the roof over my porch replaced once and I could see by eye that the new pitch was going in the wrong direction. I checked the carpenter's level with my master and guess what? Even though he had only bought it a few days before, it was off just enough to cause the problem. (Sure, he could have dropped it.) I have not found many like that, but all it takes is one.

CAST IRON SPIRIT LEVEL AND INCLINOMETER:

Some of these cast iron levels are truly works of art, with their swirling filigree and pinstriping. Unfortunately, there are times when much of the japanning is gone, the vial is dry, and the movable dial on the inclinometer is frozen.

JAPANNING AND PINSTRIPING:

Japanning has been discussed before, but these levels have an added consideration, and that is the pinstriping. The better models have this feature and if you are going to try to re-japan, you risk covering up the pinstriping. In this case, I recommend merely enhancing the old japan. You can use the art store japan, or the real stuff (if you can get it) or smudges of the Krylon #1614. See page 111.

Wipe the existing japan clean with any soft detergent and rub the rust spots with fine steelwool until they are cleaned and no longer flaky. Then brush the new japan, or #1614, on with a small paint brush. Krylon #1614 comes in a spray can, so you will have to spray a small amount onto a pallet first. Feather it into the existing japan and let it dry a day or so if you are using real japan, or 5-10 minutes if you are using #1614.

When thoroughly dry, you can then go over everything with wax or, if you go gently enough, French polish. When finishing over a re-japanned surface, I usually use a test piece that I have japanned at the same time as the level.

The upper and lower flanges are un-japanned on their flat surfaces. They usually are rusted to some degree. They should be cleaned up with emery paper and a wire wheel. Do this before the enhancing above.

To make the level workable, you will need to break loose any screws that adjust the vials. Penetrating oil and some gentle rapping will usually do it. Disassembling the vials will make them considerably easier to clean and polish.

VIAL REPLACEMENT:

If you have to replace a vial, you will first have to take it out of its brass cylinder cover. Some horizontal covers have removable ends, while the vertical covers are open ended. Dig out the old plaster and position the new vial with plaster-of-paris, or spackling paste.

The models with vial cylinders are factory adjusted, and as long as the cylinder has not been damaged, it should go back into a level position. Those models with vials similar to wooden levels will have to be adjusted in the manner described on page 82.

INCLINOMETERS:

Inclinometer models have a few more things that need to be taken care of: the half-moon section that houses the movable vial must be free to turn, the adjusting screws (on some models) must be free also, and the tiny pointer on the face of the inclinometer dial should be present and not frozen to the dial.

This latter repair requires jeweler's screwdrivers and a lot of patience. The three tiny screws that attach the circular dial should be removed along with the screw holding the pointer. This is not always easy, and you stand a chance of snapping off the screws if they are seriously corroded. Of course they can be drilled out and replaced, but that's not easy either.

I suggest that you give it a try with some penetrating oil soaking overnight. And if that doesn't work, get some oil to the half moon section and try to get it to move without disassem-

84

bling it. If all that doesn't work, and you *have* to replace the vial, drill out the screws.

If you are missing a pointer, or the one on the inclinometer is so bad that it should be replaced, ask around at one of the club meetings. There was a dealer who sold them, and the screws too.

TRY SQUARES AND BEVELS

Unless you are dealing with a combination bevel & square, there is not much to do to get these tools looking good. The one most likely drawback is when the blade is pitted. The more valuable squares or bevels would warrant some effort to remove the pitting, but the more common models are best gotten rid of as-is if they are severely pitted.

When the blade shows some evidence of the original bluing I'd leave it alone, unless there are some bad rust spots here and there. I would opt for an emery and steelwool job if that were the case.

You have to be careful with the emery on a square, because it's tough to get at the area where the blade joins the wood handle. The tendency is to use the emery *along* the longitudinal dimension of the handle, which is perpendicular to the blade. It will show up as a hack job when you're done if you do this. You must stay with the longitudinal dimension of the *blade* no matter how close to the handle you are.

If you wrap the emery paper around the blade of a knife and then use it starting from the handle and going toward the end of the blade, you will blend with any other marks left on the blade. Keep changing to finer and finer grit and finish with steelwool. Don't use the wire wheel because it will give you the same crosshatch effect as above. See Fig.36.

The wood and the brass should be cleaned and finished as described on pages 100 and 107.

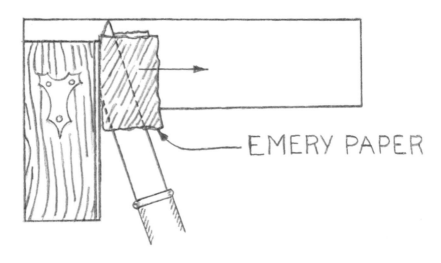

EMERY PAPER

Figure 36

CALIPERS, DIVIDERS AND COMPASSES

With the exception of some cooper's dividers (usually called compasses), log calipers, and wooden trammel points, most other tools of this group are iron; later models are of steel. Many of them need to be cleaned of their rust, and made movable with a little oil.

The biggest problem is a missing wingscrew. If the piece is valuable, you should take one from your box of spare parts that you have been accumulating from your flea market trips. If it is common, just throw *it* in the box.

Log calipers with a "pinwheel" to measure the log length are very valuable. They are worth putting some effort into getting the wood clean, the brass untarnished, and the pinwheel with all its parts.

The most common missing part on the pinwheel is the ferrule. Of the 10 spokes on the wheel, there could be as many as three or four ferrules missing. In most cases, it just means finding some brass tubing of the correct diameter and cutting it to size. If that's not possible, you can always have the ferrules made. I know wood turners who can turn them on a wood lathe!

86

Some people have replaced the missing ferrules with cartridge shells. Clever, but no-go. Whenever possible (and within economic limits) a reproduction should look like the original.

There is an argument that says that reproduced parts should *not* look like the originals, so as to identify them as *reproduced.* Collectors accepting this theory should be happy with the bullet shells. But I haven't found many people that will opt for the bullet shells rather than the professionally turned ferrules. The turned ones look exactly like the remaining originals, and as far as I'm concerned, that's the definition of a good reproduction.

TRAMMEL POINTS

Brass or steel points usually need to be cleaned and polished. However, it is common for them to be missing their keepers, or pressure protection plates, that keep the tightening screw from cutting into the wooden beam. It's not likely that you will want to spend the time to make one identical to the cast pieces that were factory made.

Normally all that is done is that a strip of brass is bent twice to form the "U" keeper. Round the ends slightly to give it a better look. I like to have both keepers the same, so if one original is still with the beam (not very likely) I replace both. The original goes in my box of parts and will someday match another set of trammels with one keeper missing. See Fig.37.

Wooden trammel points also may be missing one or two keepers, but in addition are prone to having a missing steel point and ferrule. Unless they are pretty snappy points, I wouldn't bother making a ferrule. A point can be made from a nail that is the right diameter. If a ferrule must be had, see page 86 regarding replaced ferrules. The keepers and thumb-screws are sometimes eliminated in place of wooden wedges similar to the wedges on slide arm plows.

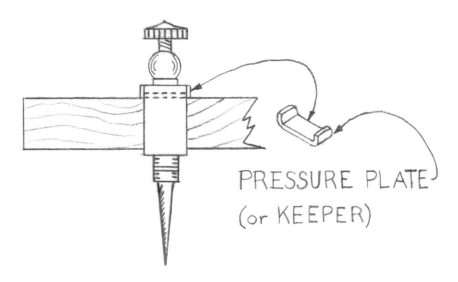

PRESSURE PLATE
(or KEEPER)

Figure 37

GAUGES AND SLITTERS

Aside from cleaning the brass and the wood, these tools are sometimes in need of a keeper (see trammel points, page 87) a thumbscrew, and a scribing point. Thumbscrews are another part that will come out of your parts box. Some are wood, some are metal, but when you need one it's great to have it available in your parts box. There are a few very expensive mortise gauges that might be worth having one made if you can't find one in your box. Scribing points can be just thin nails cut to length.

The mortise bar (the one that controls the movable point) should go in and out freely in order to move the point. Broken joints on the more complicated gauges can be re-soldered to make them functional. Soldering is a frustrating business if you don't have the right consistency solder, the right flux, the proper size iron or torch etc. If you've never done it before, go see your friend and learn how.

Slitters will have their blade missing more often than not. A piece of a straight razor or small file ground to size would be correct, but a strip of regular steel will also do.

In the classic leatherworker's slitter with the trigger grip, both the slitting blade and the L-plate between the blade and the locking screw are usually missing. Look to see if the U-keeper behind the thumbscrew that locks the bar is there. That has a tendency to get lost also.

As this piece is a specialty tool, it pays to copy from one that is complete. If you want to do the job right, that plate and keeper will take a lot of file work. You can "cheat" by just making them flat. At least it will be usable.

TRAVELERS

Not much work has to be done on travelers. Most of the factory models can be disassembled, wire wheeled, and reassembled. Then they can be repainted, if they were painted originally. The handforged models should be lightly cleaned and made to turn freely. The handle can be treated similar to chisel handles, see page 27. If the piece is old, be sure that you make the handle look the part.

SAWS

Today, most saws are restored to be put into collections, not to be used. Occasionally, hand saws are set and filed, and blades replaced in jeweler's, coping, and keyhole saws. Sawing timbers, logs etc. is hard work, and is done with power in this age. For that matter, most carpentry work is done with power saws of one kind or another.

Where a restorer will usually sharpen a blade in a plane, he will most likely leave the teeth in a saw dull and with little set. It goes against the rule of how a prideful worker would keep it, but I suppose there have to be exceptions to all rules.

TWO-MAN SAWS

TIMBER AND VENEER SAW:

Heavy cross-cut saws, plank saws, pit saws, and veneer saws need some thought before cleaning the blade. If the blade is completely oxidized, you should not abrade it with wire wheels or emery. If you break through the patina, it will look blotchy and worse than before. Steelwool and oil is best, and doesn't take a great amount of effort.

Some of the later-date saws will have their blades in reasonable shape and can be cleaned up to remove what rust is there, by abrading. The handles and the wood frames can be cleaned and refinished if needed. See page 100.

Open pit saws have two handles; the upper one (called the tiller) is usually with the saw. The lower one (called the box) is almost always missing. If you want to have the saw complete, you will have to make a box, as they are rarely found alone.

Fig.38 shows the most common type of box. It will fit any open pit saw. These lower handles were continually taken off and put back on again as part of the procedure of pit sawing. (It was the only way to reinsert the blade into the cut when the cross piece that supported the log was moved along and blocked the cut.)

I imagine these boxes were left out overnight wherever they were laid at the end of the day. Consequently, what few are found are wormy, rotted and banged up. Those in that condition could be helped with wood hardener, epoxy and filler. The wedge holding the handle onto the blade is a separate piece as shown in Fig.38.

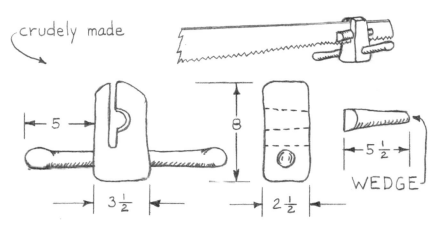

Figure 38

Pit saws got hard use. As the tiller will probably be beat up, I suggest distressing the new box to match its look. Distressing a newly reproduced part is a point of contention amongst collectors. A few feel that it is some form of "dishonesty". If you feel any twinges in this respect, merely stamp, carve or burn the date into the piece in some inconspicuous place. It's a lot better than having a "naked" out-of-sync look to the part.

ONE-MAN, TWO-HANDED SAWS

ICE SAW:

Ice saws are similar to open pit saws, but do not have a *lower* handle. (Holding your breath under the icy water must have been too much for even our hardiest pioneers.) Their blades are black with oxidation and should be left alone as mentioned above for pit saws.

BUCK AND BOW SAW:

Buck saws and bow saws, aside from needing some life put back into the wood (with tung oil) are sometimes missing their toggle or tightening stick and the cord that holds the saw together. You can get quite creative with the shape of the toggle stick, but the simpler shape is shown in Fig.39.

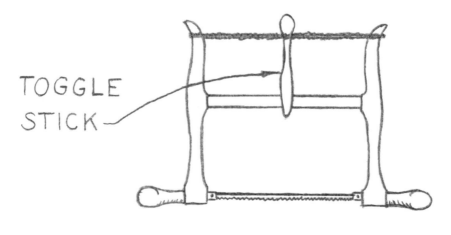

TOGGLE STICK

Figure 39

You might want to stain the white cord to give it the proper aged look. Don't make the toggle stick any longer than just reaching the tension bar. Then you won't have to struggle with each turn of the toggle to get it passed the bar.

If you must knot the cord, make the knot small. Sometimes the end of the cord is just put between the regular twist of the rest of the cord. The trouble with that is it's not permanent. If you prefer the neatness of the no-knot style, you can put a dab of glue at the end of the cord. Of course that defeats the purpose of the no-knot method, which is to adjust the toggle to come out exactly tight enough on the last turn — but it's neat.

TURNING AND FELLOE SAW:

These saws usually show a warpage of their arms. You can get it out by taking the saw apart and steam bending the warped piece true. Not many collectors care to spend the effort to do this, as these saws are hardly ever used today. They will need life breathed back into the wood as the buck saws above.

If the frame is loose, tighten the nut at the end of the blade extender. If the nut is frozen, use penetrating oil and a gentle back and forth motion until it breaks loose.

If it won't come loose because it is corroded into the threaded extender, you might want to hacksaw the nut off across its face (but not through the threaded extender). If you cannot find another nut that will fit, you can rethread the extender. It will probably need it anyway.

If the frame is loose because the original nut is bottomed out to the thread of the extender, then all that is needed is a washer or two under the nut.

STAIR SAW:

Stair saws with missing blades are normally corrected by cutting a piece of an old cross-cut hand saw for the blade. You might have to make the original line of cut with a small grinder from a Dremel tool. Then put the blade in a vise and snap it off to the line. If you don't want to bother with that, or if you don't have the Dremel tool, you can torch the temper out of the blade, keeping the heat away from the teeth. It will then be easier to hacksaw and drill.

ONE-HANDED SAWS

HAND SAW:

Hand saws (cross-cut and rip) are the most common of saws, and today are one of the most common tools found in flea markets. I suppose that's because most carpenters use power saws, even on the site. However, there are quite a few of the older saws that are collectible, due to rare signatures and shapely handles. These handles have such a nice feel that it's a shame that new saws today don't copy these older patterns.

Older saws have little finish left on their handles, making these handles relatively easy to clean. But the later saws with heavy flaking varnish puts the collector back in the decision making mode. Do I take off all the finish and do it over, or do I amalgamate the flaking finish into a homogeneous one with some alcohol or strippers? Be advised that taking *all* the finish off of a *thickly* varnished or shellacked handle is not fun. But amalgamation doesn't always end up easy either. What a rotten set of options.

The blade is also pesky. To clean the blade it should first be disassembled from the handle. Early saws used "split screws", which were really screws with slotted nuts. They can be removed with a two-pronged spanner tool. They can also be removed with needle-nose pliers set into the slots like a spanner. Later saws had dome-headed nuts with slots fully across. They can be removed with a regular screwdriver.

Almost any grit of emery that has enough abrasiveness to cut through rust will scratch the blade. You are now faced with the necessity of going finer and finer with the grit of the emery until the scratches are gone. Then a fine wire wheel or steelwool will finish it off and give a smooth bright surface.

BUT, you might have taken off some, or all, of the engraving on the blade! In many cases, the engraving is what determines the value of the saw. With patience, there is a way to do it without ruining the engraving.

Pick off any flakes of rust with a tiny pick where they are in an area of engraving. You can go over the engraved area with some fine emery on a *flat block*, watching that you do not remove any of the engraving. Be sure the blade is on a flat surface when you do this. The rest of the blade can be emeried to match.

When you are dealing with grits over 400, the paper will load up quickly if you use it dry. You will have to add oil to keep from constantly changing to new paper. Practice on a worthless saw first. Maybe you won't like the way it comes out. In that case, just oil the blade and forget it.

BACK SAW:

Miter saws, tenon saws and dovetail saws are restored very much like the hand saws above. They just aren't as much work.

METAL CUTTING SAW:

Jeweler's saws and hack saws take some wire wheel work and some refinishing of the handle. Penetrating oil will break loose the wingscrews and nuts that tighten the blade. A new blade is a must for these saws.

SHARPENING SAWS:

If you really want to have a saw sharpened and set, give it to a pro. There are shops all over that do sharpening at a reasonable price. However, there are some carpenters of the old school who will not let their saws be sharpened with a wheel as done by today's pros. There are also a few collectors (not many) that love to sharpen. Most collectors will not have their *valuable* saws sharpened, as it removes part of the history and narrows down the blade.

SAWSETS

These are fascinating mechanisms and take little work to get them in shape, although I doubt that many collectors will ever use them. They are easy to disassemble, wire wheel and oil. If they were originally painted, they can be repainted before oiling. The occasional wooden handle can be refinished as per page 100.

Very often some of the many parts of the more complicated sawsets are missing. Check with Todd Friberg's *Patented American Sawsets*, Osage Press, (published by the author).

OTHER TOOLS

TAPS AND SCREWBOXES

TAP:

Taps are simple to clean. A wire wheel will usually do it, with some oil afterwards. If you have intentions to use the tap, don't use the wire wheel, as it tends to roll over the edge. But so few of the older taps are anywhere near usable that I hardly think you will be concerned about the cutting edge.

Taps that were designed to be used in the end grain are worthwhile to get into working condition. A small 3-cornered stone and a small tapered round stone are what you will need to sharpen them.

SCREWBOX:

Screwboxes are a little more difficult, as they require disassembly to orient and sharpen the blade. Most of them will come apart when removing the two screws that hold the top and bottom pieces together. Some boxes, might have threaded wooden dowels in place of the screws.

Once the pieces are apart, loosen the bolt that holds the blade in place. Clean and sharpen the blade and reassemble the screw box. Getting the blade correctly set will take some fiddling and testing. You can finish the wood as described on page 100.

HAMMERS AND MALLETS

The most common problem with these tools is a simple one to fix: a loose head. Usually all that is needed is to slam the bottom of the hammer handle straight down on a hard surface. This will force the head down tighter on the handle, at least temporarily.

For a more permanent fix, drive a steel wedge down the top eye opening of the hammer into the handle. If it is a very early hammer that you are not going to use, the temporary fix above is more appropriate.

If you can get the head off before tightening, do it. Now the head can be easily cleaned on a soft wire wheel. If it won't come off, be careful that you don't scuff the wooden handle with the wire wheel. Use steelwool in those spots where the head meets the handle. Treat the wood as described on page 100. The head should be oiled.

CLAMPS AND VISES

CLAMP:

Wooden parallel clamps should be disassembled so that the threaded arms can be cleaned and made to run smoothly in the jaws. You might have to do a little sanding and filing as described on page 52. A good stripping, staining and waxing of the wood will help the appearance of the clamp.

There is at least one collector I know who collects these clamps as a specialty, and has written a few articles describing them. However, they are purchased mostly to use.

Later-style clamps, with threaded metal rods, are much easier to disassemble and clean. They are more sought after by users than the all-wooden ones.

Metal C-clamps are not very collectible but quite effective in use. The quick-release type is the easiest to clean and the easiest to use. The most often missing part on these clamps is the swiveled shoe at the end of the threaded rod. Without this shoe, the clamp is hardly worth restoring, considering how cheap they are in the flea markets. Wire wheeling or steelwool and oil is all that is needed for these tools.

VISE:

Metal vises are collectible if ornate — and usable if plain but functional. Sometimes the springs which hold the jaws open are missing. These are easy to replace if you can find the right material (flat spring steel). Unless there are obvious rust spots, all that is generally needed is a good oiling.

Wooden vises have as their main problem: the binding of the threaded shaft that opens and closes the vise. Correct this as you would a screw-arm plow plane, per page 52.

SCREWDRIVERS

The earlier turnscrews have brass on the ferrule to polish, wood on the handle to clean and refinish, and iron or steel on the blade to wire wheel or steelwool. The later spiral-type screwdrivers of the Yankee and Stanley models, require more attention. See page 9.

WRENCHES

Most wrenches are all metal, and need to be disassembled before they are cleaned with a wire wheel and oiled. Some have wooden handles which might need to be cleaned and refinished per page 100.

Many monkey wrenches and pipe wrenches have wooden handles that are locked to the threaded body of the wrench with a *left-handed* nut at the bottom of the handle. You should try to loosen the nut with a clockwise motion first, before turning it the standard way.

TOOL CHESTS

Restoration of a tool chest takes skills almost as good as those of the original maker. As I stated in the Introduction, this book can't cover *all* woodworking skills. There are quite a few books on the market that can do this much better than this one.

In short, these chests usually can stand some cleaning up, gluing up, and tightening up.

Aside from these tasks, you might find a need to repair the veneer inside the box. This is an art that is hard to get from a book. There are certain *basic* repair techniques: loosen the veneer with a hot iron, glue it back (in some cases with a hypodermic needle specially made for gluing), or surgically cut out the damaged section and replace it with an exact profiled new section. They all take practice, but when you finish up a veneer repair, there is a sense of satisfaction that is tops in the restoration business.

I suggest that you talk to a woodworker experienced in veneering before you start on a project of this nature. In fact, whenever you find a restoration technique that you haven't done before, you're always better to consult a friend who has done it. Even if he is not good at it, he can give you some pointers as to *what not to do.*

In restoration as in life, a friend is your best way to learn. And if you're lucky enough to have such a friend with experience and an ability to teach, you will be a restorer in no time.

CLEANING AND REFINISHING

This last section is devoted to the general cleaning and refinishing of materials that are commonly found in antique tools: wood, brass, iron, steel, and ivory. Horn, tortoise shell, mother of pearl, and other similar materials are used so rarely in tools that they are omitted from this section. There is not much that you can do with them anyhow.

I feel that it is worthwhile to repeat the concept of restoring that this book is based on: **An antique tool should be in the same condition today as it was in the hands of a prideful worker a hundred or so years ago.**

Sometimes it's a little difficult to stick to this exactly. There are going to be times, when for aesthetic reasons, you will bring up a finish just a bit more than it ever was. And you may wish to leave the dirt and grime on a very valuable old tool so as not to disturb any history that might be hidden in that schmutz.

WOOD

CLEANING:

There are varying degrees of aggressiveness in cleaning any material — wood being one that has quite a few. Soap and water is perhaps the simplest, but in most cases it hardly does the job, and it raises the grain. Household cleaners are easier to use and more efficient then plain soap and water, and they raise the grain less.

Years ago, linseed oil and turpentine, combined in grandfather's secret formula (which was darn near any combination at all) was the "cat's meow" of cleaners. I dislike it because of the lingering smell. However, it does accomplish cleaning and preserving at one time, and for that I give it Honorable Mention.

If you really want to get off dirt, paint, tar, varnish, and almost any other surface ugliness, strippers are the best. I am excluding deep oil, ink or other stains that will be discussed later.

Don't squinch up your nose at the thought of strippers. Like anything else they have to be used in the proper place and in the proper way. There is a theory that once the patina is taken off of wood it can't be brought back. If you wish to consider the true meaning of the word patina, which is, "any thin coating or color change *resulting from age*," then I would have to say there is some truth in the theory.

But you *can* get the color change back, and to some degree even the thin coating. It won't be original, and that's where you have to make some compromises. Is it better for that wonderful tool to look like it's been on the floor of a barn with 100 years of crud on it, or better for it to be cleaned with a new finish that looks like it did years ago? I don't have any problem with that decision.

STRIPPERS:

With today's chemical products, you better know what's in them. The strippers that are the most effective unfortunately contain some bad stuff like: methanol, toluene, and the really wicked guy—methylene chloride. I used these strippers with a *double vapor filter* mask for many years, thinking that I was protected.

When my lungs were hurting and my breathing was impaired, I went to a doctor. I didn't smoke so that couldn't have caused the problem. To cut short the story, I found at the bottom of the sheet that was included with the mask (in print so small that you had to use a magnifying glass): DO NOT USE THIS MASK WITH METHYLENE CHLORIDE. USE A FULL FACE MASK WITH SEPARATE AIR SUPPLY. Lucky for me nature has a way to heal lungs that are not too far gone, and I am OK today.

What is the moral of this story? Is it to never use a stripper with methylene chloride? As far as *I'm* concerned it is. 3M makes a stripper without the "bad guys", which they appropriately call *SAFEST STRIPPER*. Although the label claims that it can be used without gloves, I use them and a mask besides. It does work slower than the MC strippers, but for what we do in tool restoration I say it works good enough.

If you must use MC strippers, then consider your ventilation as an extremely important factor. If you use these strippers in a well-ventilated area (with a fan drawing the air away from you) you will probably not experience the problem that I had. But you will need a *good* mask and gloves.

These new strippers (I prefer the gel type) can be applied differently than the directions shown on the can. They can be put to work right after their application with #3 steelwool. You have complete control that way. Tools don't have heavy layers of paint on them that require the strippers to sit there and churn away for hours. It's only a thin layer of grime that you're trying to remove. These strippers attack something that benign almost immediately.

If you don't get it all off on the first pass, just go over it again. When you're done, use 0000 steelwool *dry*. It tends to lay down any grain that raised up, though this is usually not a problem. When the grime is light, I use the stripper on 0000 steelwool on the first pass. On very light grime, I use the steelwool dry.

I have been using these strippers for about 25 years and have never used a neutralizer. I believe that only lye-based strippers need a neutralizer. I will admit that the 3M stripper does leave a slight residue, but a damp rag and steelwool takes it right off. Of all the tools that I have refinished, I've never seen any bad reaction that resulted from not neutralizing.

If you dislike strippers of any kind, you can use steel wool dry — #3 first and then 0000. It's not as fast, and takes more elbow grease, but you will be surprised how the life will come back into an otherwise "dead" looking tool.

BLEACHING:

This is a sensitive process used to remove stubborn stains. It is questionable at its best. Used incorrectly, it can do more harm than good, as it is difficult to reverse if it's over-done. If you want to give it a try, start with oxalic acid in pow-der form from the hardware store and follow the directions. Oxalic acid bleach works reasonable well for iron stains, but might not be powerful enough for other types of stains.

You might have to use a 2-part wood bleach. It *will* get the stain out, but in order to keep from going from the frying pan into the fire, i.e. from a dark spot to a *very* light spot, you will almost have to bleach the entire piece and then stain it back. As I said above, it is sensitive and questionable. Unless stains really bother you, stay away from bleaching.

FILLING CRACKS AND VOIDS:

I have heard opposition to filling cracks and holes by explaining that a prideful worker of years ago would never bother to fill these "defects". He would not even consider them as defects, merely part of the use and aging process. That's a tough one to argue against. I'm going to dodge behind the "exception to the rule" hedge. As I said previously, aesthetics can color one's concept of how a tool should look "in the hands of a prideful worker".

OK, that's over with; now let's fill There are a good many fillers on the market. I suppose it depends on personal choice. I like *PLASTIC WOOD* (Bondex, St. Louis, MO), because it dries fast and hard. It comes in colors too. Three col-ors I use are: natural for boxwood, oak for birch and beech, and walnut for darker woods. I also mix oak and walnut where needed. You will have to experiment around no matter what brand you use.

Bear in mind that stain will take differently depending upon how much time the filler is allowed to dry, and it will more than likely darken the spot more than you planned on.

You can also fill with sawdust (from the wood) mixed with glue. This will definitely take some practice. You have to pack the dust and glue into a very tight consistency or it will dry porous. And you may have to sand it lightly to accept stain.

Maybe I'm just lazy, but I have always had better luck with the "store-bought" fillers.

Where you have a deep crack or wide chip, you will have to build up the fill. I try to fill the entire crack, if possible. Allow time for drying between applications. And follow the directions, as each manufacturer has different build-up allowances and drying times.

STAINING:

Improper staining can destroy an otherwise magnificent restoration. It seems very easy when you watch them do it on TV. The difference is they don't have to *match* a wedge to a 200-year-old molding plane, or the tip of a handle to the rest of a plow plane.

There are a variety of stains available on the market. I started with oil stains, which are OK, but take a while to dry and don't usually penetrate the tight-grained woods. So I swung over to aniline dyes which are pretty good penetrants, and dry in less than a minute. Don't sweat the word *aniline*. I hear that there is no real aniline in these dyes. The term is only a generic description of synthetic dyestuffs.

If you are going to do very much restoring that will require stain, experiment with aniline powder stains from *MOHAWK* (Amsterdam, NY). I use three colors: dark red mahogany, medium brown walnut, and extra dark walnut. I also have a yellow left over from years ago that I use only rarely (to give a yellow hue to English beech, boxwood etc.).

Alcohol-base anilines are very fast drying, but not totally light-fast. Water-base anilines are slower drying but are reasonably light fast. Mohawk has a new powder than will work with both their reducer (in place of alcohol) and also with water.

If you only have a few small jobs to do and don't want to spend the money for the aniline powder and reducer, try some *SOLAR-LUX* (Behlen's Amsterdam, NY). It is a methanol stain and dries in about 30 minutes. A warning: *chronic methanol exposure is dangerous.*

If you just want a ½ pint of oil stain from the hardware store, try MINWAX (Montvale, NJ). It dries in 24 hours.

It's rare that you will be able to match anything that you are doing right out of one can. You're going to have to mix and match and test on sample pieces. Even then you might find it goes on the real piece just a bit darker or lighter and you will have to adjust after the first try.

If it's too light, add some darker stain to the mix and try that. If it's too dark, steelwool some off and start over. If you are using penetrants, you might have to resort to alcohol if it's too dark. It goes without saying that you are better off too light than too dark on your first pass.

Many restorers will put a final coat of stain on the entire piece once the restored part is matched as well as can be expected. It tends to put the same sheen on everything. If there is nothing to match, and you are merely replacing the color that you feel the plane had years ago, the whole staining process is much easier.

If you get a blotchy effect, you can spot in the lighter spots with a paintbrush with darker stain, or lighten up some of the darker spots with steelwool rubbed with the tip of a screwdriver or the eraser-end of a pencil.

I like to burnish *new* wood after staining. It closes up the grain and gives it a smoother "handled" look. If you have to burnish the *old* wood to match, do it. I use a tapered hardened rod, but almost anything, even the round portion of a screwdriver blade, will work.

FINISHING:

The hard part is over. Now all you have to do is put on the finish coat of oil, wax, or French polish. I left out varnish, as it only looks right on a tool that is brand new. You can simulate an aged varnish coat for older planes by distressing, but it's too much trouble for what you get out of it. Whatever you do, stay away from polyurethane. It gives a plastic looking finish.

OIL:

Oiling a wooden part is easy, looks good, and *is* good for the preservation of the wood. Boiled linseed oil will do the job, but it does have a lingering smell and it encourages mildew (although the mildew wipes off as easy as dust). Tung oil will penetrate deeper and will not hold an odor as long. Don't leave the part drenched or the tung oil will end up sticky. A few light coats rubbed in will not only provide life for the wood but will give it a sheen.

WAX:

Wax is a good coating, as it fills small cracks and holes and gives the wood a nice look. It can be used on the metal also, just as oil can. Any of the paste waxes will work. I like the dark variety of *MINWAX*. It deepens the tone of the wood.

FRENCH POLISH:

French polishing is almost a lost art. Instead of going into the details of how to French polish the real way, I will give you the shortcut. Mohawk makes a product called *LACOVER*. It goes on almost like the real thing, and ends up looking like it. They make two varieties of it: #30 and #50. The latter puts on a heavier coating, but it is harder to use on a large surface. There aren't very many tools with surfaces large enough to cause any problems (except maybe tool boxes) so I use #50.

If you don't like it, you can always thin it down with the solvent that Mohawk supplies. Here's the trick in using it:

LACOVER works by friction. If you put too much of it on the cotton rubbing pad, it will just run over the surface you are putting it on and not polish. If it is too dry, it won't do anything at all. So, after soaking the pad, damp it off on another pad and wait a few seconds before starting to rub.

After a second or two it will start to get a little sticky. That's when you have to ease off on the pressure or you will just "pick up" whatever *LACOVER* has been laid down. Most of the time it works best in a circular motion, but never let the pad stand still. If you want more shine, just put on another coat.

The tighter grained woods, like ebony and boxwood take a more delicate touch. You should practice until you get the "feel" of it. You can't make a mistake as it comes off with 0000 steelwool or the solvent. You might find it easier to put a light coat of oil on the wood before polishing.

French polish is not the finish for all tools. Not by a long shot. There must be a smooth, almost burnished surface to the wood or you are wasting your time.

BRASS, BRONZE AND GUNMETAL

CLEANING:

There are brass cleaners in the hardware store such as *BRASSO* (R.T. French Co., Rochester, NY) and *NEVR-DULL* (George Basch Co., Freeport, NY) that do a nice job if the piece is not heavily corroded. However, when the oxidation is tough to get off, you might have to use more abrasive techniques.

One that not too many people believe can be done without marring the piece is with a wire wheel! There are wire wheels that are made with *brass* wires no thicker than a human hair. They are usually mounted on a wooden spindle that can be drilled out to fit any shaft. They are available at some factory supply houses. I have found that if I don't press the work into the wheel too hard, I can even use a fine *steel* wire wheel to get most of the corrosion off. The trick is not to get into the brass itself. Some oxidation should be left when you change over to polishing on the rag wheel.

There are chemicals that can be wiped on the brass that will almost work on their own, as long as you keep them wet. *METAL CARE* (Woodcare Corp., New Castle, VA) makes this type. Whenever you use a product of this kind on brass, it should be flushed off with water after it has done its job. Most of these products require that you polish afterward.

One of the disadvantages of this type of cleaner is that it runs over the entire piece and strips the corrosion everywhere. Most restorers like to leave the crevice areas alone. These are the areas that would be oxidized normally, but would never be cleaned by usage. This gives it a deeper two-toned look, which is more like it would have been.

Extremely heavy corrosion can be attacked with fine emery paper (320 grit), followed by crocus or jeweler's cloth. Remove any remaining scratches on the rag wheel. See the instructions under POLISHING below.

POLISHING

Some collectors do not like shiny brass; others love it. You can leave some of the finer oxidation on all areas if you like, but my personal preference is to polish areas that would have been naturally polished by the craftsman's hand through daily usage.

Rag wheels can be purchased in almost any hardware store, but I go to the larger stores to be sure. Six-inch wheels are fine for the usual $\frac{1}{3}$ to $\frac{1}{2}$ HP motors. Use two of them together as they are generally only $\frac{1}{2}$" thick.

My motor runs at 1725 RPM but you can use a spindle with a belt and pulleys to change the speed upward. Of course you can use a 3450 RPM motor, but you will need more finesse at that speed so that you don't burn the polish.

I only use two polishes: tripoli (beige) and jeweler's rouge (red). The red rouge brings it to a high polish and I don't use it as much, only when I am trying to make the tool something that it really wasn't — a showpiece. (Yes, this is another exception to my rule.)

Tripoli is abrasive, but with very little scratching. It does the job for most everything. You should wash off the polished surface to get rid of any residue. If you want to "fix" the finish so it doesn't tarnish again, you might French polish it or work it over with rubbing lacquer. This will dull it a little so you will have to compromise here.

If you prefer a more natural look to the brass, *don't* "fix" it. In a month or two it will oxidize slightly and lose some of that luster from the polishing wheel. If you want to dampen that luster immediately, rub it with your hand, or a rough rag until you have it the way you want it. You can always take the luster off completely with some 0000 steelwool and start over.

A word of caution about using a rag wheel or a wire wheel: They will kick a small piece right out of your hand, and you will waste a lot of time looking for it on the floor. *Do not* turn a small piece while it is held against the wheel. Back off a bit, turn it, and then proceed against the wheel. This might be slower, but you will never be on your hands and knees looking for it.

I am assuming that you *always* put on your safety glasses when you are using a wire wheel or even a rag wheel. A face shield is better. With the wire wheel, it's the pieces of wire that fly out of the wheel that can seriously injure your eyes.

IRON AND STEEL

CLEANING:

Very old iron tools are usually found with a dark brown, almost black patina (a deeper form of iron oxide — Fe_3O_4). This is an excellent coating to prevent the lighter red rust (Fe_2O_3),from forming, and should be just rubbed with oil — nothing more.

Heavy red rust can be broken down with a coarse wire wheel and finished off with a fine one. My motor has a double-ended shaft that allows me to have both coarse and fine on the same motor. It is quite convenient. Most all cleaning should be done with the finer wheel if the piece merely needs a little work.

Very heavy rust might need to be "chiseled" off, then emeried, and *then* wire wheeled. Everyone has their own "best way", and you will find yours after a few sessions with a heavily rusted part.

That brings up the subject of pitting. Most of the time there is nothing that can be done to remove it entirely. If the pits are *tiny* they can be sanded or ground out. In any case, you can polish the area with the fine wire wheel to take away the "found in a dung heap" look.

A warning: some steel, such as on the cap iron of a metal plane, will matte easily if you work it over too much, even with a fine wheel. You will notice a lighter color "blotch" where you have broken through the skin of the part. If this doesn't bother you, then make the entire surface look like it.

As the original surface never looked like this, I prefer to get rid of the error by emery papering the entire surface followed by wire wheeling with a lighter touch or a softer wheel. Polishing on a rag wheel also will help get the original look back.

There will be times when you have to wire wheel or emery a deeply oxidized surface, due to red rust spots. If you inadvertently break completely through the patina and create a shiny spot, here's how to get rid of it:

Apply gun blueing or gun browning, *PERMA BLUE* or *PLUM BROWN* (Birchwood Casey, Eden Prairie, MN) to the spot. Just follow the directions. You can get it as dark as you like with repeated applications. It might not be a perfect reversal, but it will do.

ELECTROLYTIC CLEANING:

There is an electrolytic process that will take off rust by bathing the piece in a chemical solution, while connecting it electrically. I've never used this technique, although I have seen it done and observed the results. For me, it has a few disadvantages, namely:

1) It requires equipment that is not readily available to everyone, (a battery charger) and

2) It cleans *everything*, which if you are not careful, leaves a homogeneous matte that is not natural. There should be some dirt and oxidation left in the grooves and crevices, just as there would be during regular usage. I have seen some users of this technique selectively clean only certain areas, but this is far more time consuming and doesn't work for grooves and crevices.

I think this system was developed because of a fear of wire wheels. But, if wire wheels are used as suggested earlier, it should eliminate the need for electrolytic cleaning. Yes, I doubt I will ever convince those who presently use this technique to abandon it, because it is less risky than wire wheels (you can't overdo it electrolytically), and some people prefer the homogeneous finish.

FINISHING:

When you finish cleaning iron or steel, and you don't intend to paint or japan it, you can lightly oil the part with a machine oil. I use *3-IN-ONE* (Boyle-Midway, NYC). No reason — other than my father used it.

JAPANNING OR PAINTING:

Most iron parts *that don't belong to metal planes* can be repainted with almost any black semi-gloss paint. The one that I use is *KRYLON High Heat Black #1614* (Sherwin-Williams, Solon, OH). It comes in a spray can, which makes it easy to use. The only extra effort required is to mask off the non-paint areas with standard masking tape. Don't use duct tape; it's too hard to get off. And don't forget to take the tape off before baking.

It only takes 5 or 10 minutes to dry, and you can spray on a second, or even a third coat. Naturally, the surface that you are going to paint has to be clean. Feather out any paint that is not going to be taken off so that there are no ridges when the new paint goes on. If you want, you can bake it for an hour or so at 250 to 300 degrees, which tends to harden it.

Make sure that you do your spraying in a well-ventilated area, as #1614 contains toluene.

If it comes out too shiny, you can rub it down with your hand, a rag, or even some 0000 steelwool. If it is too dull, you can French polish it or wax it.

Purists do no like to paint metal plane parts that were originally japanned. If the japanning is not that bad, all that should be done is to clean it with a detergent, then oil or French polish it to prevent any corrosion from returning.

But if almost all the original finish is gone and only rust remains, you should do something more than cleaning and oiling. There are japan colors in art stores that can be put on with enough coats to bring back a factory look. Follow the instructions, as they are not easy to use. They may dry too flat. In that case, wax or French polish over them to bring up the sheen.

If you want to use the same stuff that Stanley did (a tar base japan), talk to some of the tool dealers and find out if any of this type of japan is still around. It is tough to use and takes a few days to do it completely, but if you are a purist, that won't matter.

If you are not a purist and can't stand the look of the rusted metal plane, then clean it and use #1614. If you do it right, it will very closely match the original japanning. Even if you don't, it will be better than it was before, and it can be reversed (stripped off) if you want the plane to return to its previous ugly condition.

After you have refinished the plane with japan or #1614, make sure that any area that was not supposed to be japanned is still bare. You better look at the plane carefully *before* refinishing, because some of the bare spots are hard to distinguish because of the oxidation.

I don't indiscriminately refinish *all* the parts just to have the *identical* sheen. If some parts, or sections of some parts, are OK as-is, I leave them alone. That way there is evidence of what the original finish looked like. I do try to match the two finishes as best as I can, to make it a more professional job.

IVORY

Ivory is not any harder to clean than any other material. What creates the problem with ivory parts are the markings on rules that you want to keep from disappearing while you are cleaning. Slow, careful movements using only flat cleaning material will help. Stains can be scraped a bit with the tip of a razor blade or Xacto knife to get rid of the superficial ones, but the deep ones are almost impossible to get out.

Ivory can be French polished or waxed. If you are replacing an ivory tip from a plow plane arm you may wish to lightly stain it with boiling tea or dye penetrants to match the remaining tips.

There is nothing wrong with reproducing an ivory tip for a plane that had them originally. What *is* fraudulent is making a set of these tips for a plane that *never had them at all!* Many of these premier planes have their model numbers stamped on their bodies. The catalogs will tell you if that model came from the factory with ivory tips or not. Even if the number isn't on the plane, the catalog will tell you whether that company every made planes with ivory tips. Not very many makers made them.

ANTIQUING AND DISTRESSING REPRODUCED PARTS

What a touchy subject this is! I don't see anything wrong with trying to match patina and surface anomalies, particularly if you stamp the date on newly made parts.

Reproduced parts that show no likeness to the original parts are ludicrous. Antique tools represent more than just implements from the past. They transmit a *feeling* of *how things were.* They tell a serious story. — It's hard to tell a serious story looking like a clown!

IN CLOSING

Hopefully, this book will inspire the reader who had some thoughts of restoring but didn't feel capable of success. It's not that hard! Start slowly and give it a chance. Don't expect to make a silk purse out of a sow's ear on your first try. With practice (as with anything else) you will surprise yourself with your results. But, you will have to keep trying after your first few failures, particularly if some improvement is shown each time. We rarely accomplish the difficult on the first try.

Good luck with restoring. It's a wonderful hobby with truly great rewards. The satisfaction with before-and-afters is probably the greatest reward. But don't discount the economic payback of improving the value of your collection.

Go get those ratty looking artifacts and give them a new start. Watch those Phoenix birds rise out of their own ashes and live again.